VALUE ADDED TAX:
CONCEPTS, POLICY ISSUES, AND OECD EXPERIENCES

VALUE ADDED TAX: CONCEPTS, POLICY ISSUES, AND OECD EXPERIENCES

JAMES M. BICKLEY

Novinka Books
New York

Senior Editors: Susan Boriotti and Donna Dennis
Coordinating Editor: Tatiana Shohov
Office Manager: Annette Hellinger
Graphics: Wanda Serrano
Editorial Production: Vladimir Klestov, Matthew Kozlowski and Maya Columbus
Circulation: Ave Maria Gonzalez, Vera Popovic, Luis Aviles, Raymond Davis, Melissa Diaz and Jeannie Pappas
Communications and Acquisitions: Serge P. Shohov
Marketing: Cathy DeGregory

Library of Congress Cataloging-in-Publication Data
Available Upon Request

ISBN: 1-59033-592-9.

Copyright © 2003 by Novinka Books,
      An Imprint of Nova Science Publishers, Inc.
      400 Oser Ave, Suite 1600
      Hauppauge, New York 11788-3619
      Tele. 631-231-7269   Fax 631-231-8175
      e-mail: Novascience@earthlink.net
      Web Site: http://www.novapublishers.com

All rights reserved. No part of this book may be reproduced, stored in a retrieval system or transmitted in any form or by any means: electronic, electrostatic, magnetic, tape, mechanical photocopying, recording or otherwise without permission from the publishers.

The authors and publisher have taken care in preparation of this book, but make no expressed or implied warranty of any kind and assume no responsibility for any errors or omissions. No liability is assumed for incidental or consequential damages in connection with or arising out of information contained in this book.

This publication is designed to provide accurate and authoritative information with regard to the subject matter covered herein. It is sold with the clear understanding that the publisher is not engaged in rendering legal or any other professional services. If legal or any other expert assistance is required, the services of a competent person should be sought. FROM A DECLARATION OF PARTICIPANTS JOINTLY ADOPTED BY A COMMITTEE OF THE AMERICAN BAR ASSOCIATION AND A COMMITTEE OF PUBLISHERS.

Printed in the United States of America

CONTENTS

Preface ix

Chapter 1 Value-Added Tax: Concepts, Policy
Issues, and OECD Experiences 1
Summary 1
Introduction 2
Concept of a Value–Added Tax 3
Composition of Taxes: United States
    Compared to Other OECD Nations 7
Revenue Yield 8
Administrative Cost 10
Compliance 13
Equity 16
Neutrality 23
National Saving 24
Inflation 25
Balance–of–Trade 26
Size of Government 27
Intergovernmental Issues 28
Public Opinion 30
Appendix A. Credit–Invoice,
    Subtraction, and Addition Methods 31
Appendix B. Economic Effects of a
    Special VAT Treatment 35
Appendix C. Composition of Taxes 36
Appendix D. Possible Bases for a
    Value–Added Tax 38

	Appendix E. Summary Examples of Exemptions and Zero Rates	40
	Appendix F. VAT Rates by Country	41
	Appendix G. Dates of Adoption of Major State Taxes by State	45
	Appendix H. Percentage Distribution of State Tax Collections by Source Selected Fiscal Years, 1902-1992	48
	Appendix I. Federal Tax Collections by Type of Tax	51
	Appendix J. Sales Tax Rates By State	53
	Appendix K. Surveys of Public Opinion	54
	Selected Bibliography	59
Chapter 2	A Value-Added Tax Contrasted With a National Sales Tax	**63**
	Summary	63
	Most Recent Developments	64
	Background and Analysis	64
	Legislation	69
Chapter 3	Value-Added Tax as a New Revenue Source	**71**
	Summary	71
	Most Recent Developments	72
	Background and Analysis	72
	Legislation	79
Chapter 4	Value-added Tax in Canada: Background, Evaluation, and Implications for the United States	**83**
	Summary	83
	Background, Evaluation, and Implications for the United States	84
	Historical Development	85
	Evaluation of the Canadian VAT	88
	Implications for the United States	95
	Selected Bibliography	96
Chapter 5	Value-Added Tax: Revenue Estimates	**97**
	Summary	97
	Introduction	98
	VAT Base	100
	Calculation of Revenue Estimates	102

Limitations of Estimates	108
Bibliography	110
Index	**113**

PREFACE

The feasibility of levying a value-added tax (VAT) to reduce large forecast budget deficits seems to never go away. A VAT is imposed at all levels of production on the differences between firms' sales and their purchases from all other firms. A VAT is assumed to be fully shifted forward to consumers; hence, a VAT is a type of general consumption tax. The United States, does not have a broad-based, national level consumption tax and in general, relies less on consumption taxes. This book examines the concepts, issues and experiences of the value-added tax in other countries.

Chapter 1

VALUE-ADDED TAX: CONCEPTS, POLICY ISSUES, AND OECD EXPERIENCES

James M. Bickley

SUMMARY

Some Members of Congress have expressed interest in the feasibility of levying a value–added tax (VAT) to reduce large forecast budget deficits. A VAT is imposed at all levels of production on the differences between firms' sales and their purchases from all other firms. A VAT is assumed to be fully shifted forward to consumers; hence, a VAT is a type of general consumption tax. The United States, unlike other OECD countries, does not have a broad–based, national–level consumption tax and, in general, relies less on consumption taxes. The existence of a VAT in other countries does not, however, necessarily imply anything about the desirability of a U.S. VAT.

For fiscal year 1995, a broad–based U.S. VAT as a new revenue source would raise net revenue of approximately $28.2 billion for each one percent levied. Data on VATs in other OECD nations suggest that a U.S. VAT could be administered at a reasonable cost and with reasonably good compliance.

If disposable income over a one–year period is the measure of ability–to–pay, then a broad–based VAT with a single rate would be extremely regressive; that is, the percentage of disposable income paid in VAT would decrease rapidly as disposable income increases. If disposable income over a lifetime is the measure of ability–to–pay, a constant–rate VAT with a broad base and a single rate would be mildly regressive. Options do exist to reduce or eliminate this regressivity; three possible methods are exclusions and multiple rates, income tax credits, and earmarking of some revenue for increased social spending. If consumption over either a one–year period or a lifetime is the measure of ability–to–pay, a broad–based VAT with a single rate would be proportional; that is, the percentage of consumption paid in VAT would be the same as consumption increases. These options have drawbacks, however.

From an economic perspective, a major revenue source is better the greater its neutrality; that is, the less the tax alters economic decisions. A VAT is a relatively, but not completely, neutral tax. A VAT or any other tax that sharply reduces the deficit would raise the rate of national savings. But the prevailing view of economists is that neither a VAT nor any other major tax change would significantly affect households' propensities to save.

The imposition of a VAT would cause a one–time increase in this country's price level if the money supply is expanded to accommodate it, but would have no permanent effect on the inflation rate. If the United States continues its policy of flexible exchange rates, then the imposition of a VAT, compared to any other major tax increase, would not significantly affect the U.S. balance–of–trade. Empirical studies of the effect of a VAT on the size of the public sector are inconclusive. A Federal VAT would encroach on the States' primary source of revenue, the retail sales tax; but the Federal Government and the States already share many sources of revenue in relative harmony. Public opinion surveys show a preference for a VAT over higher individual income taxes.

INTRODUCTION

Large projected deficits in the Federal budget have generated congressional interest in new sources of revenue.[1] One policy option discussed has been the imposition of a value–added tax (VAT) because of its high revenue potential and widespread use by other developed nations. This chapter examines 13 aspects of a VAT relevant to the issue of levying a VAT for deficit reduction. These aspects are the concept of a value–added tax, comparison of the composition of taxes between the United States and

---

[1] For a comprehensive examination of the case for fiscal restraint, see: U.S. General Accounting Office. *Budget Policy: Prompt Action Necessary to Avert Long–term Damage to the Economy; Report to Congressional Requesters.* Washington, 1992. 116 p.

other OECD nations, revenue yield, administrative cost, compliance, equity, neutrality, national saving, inflation, balance–of–trade, size of Government, intergovernmental relations, and public opinion. This report considers the experiences of the 22 nations (out of 24 nations) with VATs in the Organization for Economic Cooperation and Development (OECD) relevant to the feasibility and operation of a U.S. VAT.[2]

CONCEPT OF A VALUE–ADDED TAX

A value–added tax is a tax, levied at each stage of production, on firms' value added. The value added of a firm is the difference between a firm's sales and a firm's purchases of inputs from other firms. In other words, a firm's value added is simply the amount of value a firm contributes to a good or service by applying its factors of production (land, labor, capital, and entrepreneurial ability).[3] Another method of calculating a firm's value added is to total the firm's payments to its factors of production.

Types of VAT

There are three types of VATs which differ in their tax treatment of purchases of capital inputs (plant and equipment). Under the *consumption VAT*, capital purchases are treated the same way as the purchase of any other input: the purchase price is deducted at the time of purchase. This tax treatment of capital purchases is equivalent to expensing. Under the *income VAT*, the VAT paid on the purchases of capital inputs is amortized (credited against the firm's VAT liability) over the expected lives of the capital inputs. Under the *gross product VAT*, no deduction for the VAT on purchases of capital inputs is allowed against the firm's VAT liability.

All 22 OECD nations with VATs use the consumption type. The consumption VAT is the type usually advocated for this country. Indeed, most VAT advocates intend to shift tax burdens from capital income to consumption. Furthermore, a consumption VAT is simpler to compute

---

[2] The OECD is an international organization dedicated to promoting international trade, economic growth, and economic stability. The OECD consists of 18 European nations, Turkey, the United States, Canada, Australia, New Zealand, and Japan.

[3] These factors of production have specific meanings to an economist. Labor consists of all employees hired by the firm. Land consists of all natural resources including raw land, water, and mineral wealth. Capital is anything used in the production process which has been made by man. The entrepreneur is the decision maker who operates the firm.

because firms do not have to separate expenditures for capital from other expenditures.

Methods of Calculating VAT

There are three alternative methods of calculating VAT: the credit method, the subtraction method, and the addition method.[4] Under the *credit method*, the firm calculates the VAT to be remitted to the Government by a two–step process. First, the firm multiplies its sales by the tax rate to calculate VAT collected on sales. Second, the firm credits VAT paid on inputs against VAT collected on sales and remits this difference to the Government. The firm calculates its VAT liability before setting its prices in order to fully shift the VAT to the buyer. Under the *credit–invoice method*, a type of credit method, the firm is required to show VAT separately on all sales invoices and to calculate the VAT credit on inputs by adding all VAT shown on purchase invoices.

Under the *subtraction method*, the firm calculates its value added by subtracting its cost of taxed inputs from its sales. Next, the firm determines its VAT liability by multiplying its value added by the VAT rate. Under the *addition method*, the firm calculates its value added by adding all payments for untaxed inputs (e.g. wages and profits). Next, the firm multiplies its value added by the VAT rate to calculate VAT to be remitted to the Government.

The credit–invoice method is used by 21 of 22 OECD nations with VATs. Tax economists differ in their classifications of the Japanese VAT. Both the credit–invoice and the subtraction methods have been discussed for the United States. The prevailing view of economists is that the credit–invoice method is superior. This method requires registered firms to maintain detailed records that are cross indexed with supporting documentation. A VAT shown on the sales invoice of one firm is the same as the VAT shown on the purchase order of another firm. Hence, the credit–invoice method allows tax auditors to cross check the records of firms. Also, each firm has a vested interest in insuring that the VAT shown on its purchase orders is not understated so the firm can receive full credit against VAT liability for VAT previously paid. Thus, the credit–invoice method could be easier to enforce. Also, the credit–invoice method is probably the only feasible method if there are to be multiple tax rates.

---

[4] Numerical examples with explanations of these three methods of calculating VAT are shown in appendix A.

Supporters of the subtraction method maintain that it would have low compliance costs because all necessary data could be obtained from records kept by a firm for other purposes. But a firm would still have to make calculations based on these data. For example, deductible expenses would have to be separated from nondeductible expenses, and some data expressed on an accrual basis would have to be converted to a cash flow basis.

The credit–invoice method would have substantial compliance costs because the amount of VAT would have to be shown on every sales invoice (and conversely on every purchase invoice). But the credit–invoice method would yield an additional data base to firms. Some firms might find these additional data useful in decision making. For example, records of purchase invoices and sales invoices may improve some firms' control over their inventories. Compliance costs of the credit–invoice method might be partially offset by the value of the VAT data base to firms, but this value has never been quantified.

The credit–invoice method would have greater administrative costs than the subtraction method because of its requirements for additional data, computations, and record–keeping. Although there are data on the administrative costs of a VAT calculated by the credit–invoice method, empirical data are not available on the subtraction method; consequently, a quantitative comparison of costs currently is not feasible. The subtraction method would not work administratively if many goods are exempt or if multiple tax rates are levied. Unless specified otherwise, this report will assume that the credit–invoice method is used and that the VAT is the consumption type.[5]

Exemption versus Zero–Rating

No VAT proposal would require all firms to collect the VAT. The two fundamental methods of giving special tax treatment to businesses in an industry under a VAT are exemption and zero–rating. An exempt business would not collect VAT on its sales and would not receive credit for VAT paid on its purchases of inputs. An exempt business would not register with tax authorities, and, consequently, would not be part of the VAT system. Hence, an exempt business would not have the usual VAT compliance costs

---

[5] For a comprehensive comparison of the credit–invoice method and the subtraction method, see: U.S. Library of Congress. Congressional Research Service. *Value–Added Tax: Should It Be Calculated by the Credit–Invoice or Subtraction Method?* Report No. 92–504 E, by James M. Bickley. Washington, 1992. 12 p.

and would not impose administrative costs on the Government (except verification of its exemption, of course). An exempt business's costs, however, include any tax paid on inputs, because it receives no credit for previously paid taxes.

A zero–rated business would not collect VAT on its sales but would receive credit for VAT paid on its inputs. This is equivalent to the business being charged a zero tax rate. A zero–rated business would be a registered taxpayer, and, consequently, would involve the usual compliance and administrative costs. A zero–rated business, however, would receive a refund of any VAT paid on its inputs, so its costs would not include VAT paid at earlier stages. The effects on final prices and total VAT collected by the Government caused by exempting or zero–rating firms would vary with the stage of production.

An exempt retailer would not charge any VAT on its sales but it would not receive any credit for VAT previously paid on its inputs, so its price to the final consumer would include all VAT paid except that on its own value–added. The Government would have collected a tax on all the value added in the product except the retailer's.

A zero–rated retailer would not charge any VAT on its sales, but it would receive credit for all VAT previously paid on its inputs. A zero–rated retailer would not remit VAT to the Government, but it would receive a refund for VAT previously paid by suppliers. Hence, the price of the commodity would not include any VAT, and the Government would receive no revenue.

Exempting or zero–rating a retailer would not affect the linkage (or chain) of VAT collections and credits between different stages of production because retailers are the final stage of production and distribution. But exempting or zero–rating an intermediate stage such as manufacturing of wholesaling would break the chain between firms at different stages of production.

Exempting, however, causes a far more serious break than zero–rating. For example, an exempt manufacturer would not collect VAT on sales to a wholesaler and would not receive credit for VAT paid on inputs. A nonexempt wholesaler would not receive credit for the VAT paid on the manufacturer's inputs included in the price it paid the manufacturer. But the wholesaler would remit VAT collected on all of its sales, so some of the value added in the product would be taxed twice. Consequently, exempting a manufacturer or any other intermediate producer would increase total VAT collected by the Government and the final retail price of the commodity.

A zero–rated manufacturer would not collect VAT on sales but would receive credit for VAT paid on inputs. The price paid by the wholesaler, therefore, would contain no VAT. The nonexempt wholesaler would collect VAT on sales and would not be eligible for any VAT credits, but the total VAT at that point would exactly equal what it would have been had there been no untaxed stage. Subsequent stages of production would charge VAT on sales and would receive credit for VAT paid on inputs as though there had been no break in the chain. Hence, zero–rating a manufacturer or other intermediate stage would change neither total VAT remitted nor the retail price on the commodity.[6]

If both zero–rated firms and exempt firms operate at the same level of production in the same industry, the zero–rated firms would have a competitive advantage, because their costs are less by the amount of the VAT.

Policy makers may be faced with a decision to either zero–rate or exempt a particular product.

> ...zero–rating is desirable when the objective is to exclude the consumption of the product completely from tax, where an exemption is warranted when it is not regarded as feasible or desirable to tax the activity but some tax on final consumption is considered desirable...
> There are two major objections to exemption. First, cascading results as the exempt firms and their business customers cannot receive input tax credit. Secondly, firms producing both exempt and taxable (including zero–rated) items must allocate inputs between exempt and non–exempt categories, and this is difficult to accomplish in any non–arbitrary way and to control.[7]

COMPOSITION OF TAXES: UNITED STATES COMPARED TO OTHER OECD NATIONS[8]

One argument frequently made for a U.S. VAT is the relative reliance on consumption taxes in other developed countries. Most other countries do in fact rely more on consumption taxes.

For fiscal year 1990, the United States (Federal, State, and local governments) relied less on all types of taxes on goods and services (16.5

---

[6] Table B1 in appendix B summarizes the selective economic effects of exemption and zero–rating which were discussed in this section.
[7] Due, John F. Some Unresolved Issues in Design and Implementation of Value–Added Taxes. *National Tax Journal*, v. 43, no. 4, December 1990. p. 385.
[8] For fiscal year 1990, the composition of taxes of each member of the OECD is shown in table C1 of appendix C.

percent of total tax revenues) than any other nation in the OECD except Japan (13.2 percent). These types of taxes on goods and services were import duties, profits on public fiscal monopolies, licenses and other business taxes, specific sales taxes, and general sales taxes. For only general taxes on goods and services (VATs, retail sales taxes, wholesale sales taxes, and manufacturers' sales taxes), the United States had a lower reliance (7.6 percent of tax revenues) than any other nation except Japan (4.2 percent of tax revenue).

For fiscal year 1990, the reliance of the United States on individual income taxes (35.8 percent of total revenue) was exceeded by only six other OECD nations. Four of these nations (Australia, Finland, New Zealand, and Sweden) did not levy social security taxes on employees. For the United States, direct taxes on employees (individual income taxes and social security taxes) accounted for a higher percentage of tax revenue (47.4 percent) than in all other OECD nations except Denmark (55.1 percent) and the Netherlands (48.2 percent).

In summary, the United States places a much higher reliance on direct taxes on employees and a much lower reliance on taxes on goods and services than most other nations in the OECD.

The adoption of a VAT by other countries does not imply that the U.S. should or should not adopt a VAT. Economic analysis of optimal taxation suggests that those choices depend on issues of efficiency, equity, and administrative costs, and should be made in the context of the overall tax and spending structure. These considerations may vary from one country to another.

REVENUE YIELD[9]

The primary reason for considering a VAT for deficit reduction is the enormous revenue potential of applying a low tax rate to a broad base.

VAT Base

The potential revenue per one percent rate from a VAT would vary with the comprehensiveness of the tax base. A broad-based VAT would have

---

[9] This section of this report updates estimates in the following source: U.S. Library of Congress. Congressional Research Service. *Value–Added Tax: Revenue Estimates for FY95*. Report No. 93–687 E, by James M. Bickley. Washington, 1993. 13 p.

limited exclusions, while a narrow–based VAT would have numerous exclusions. Obviously, the broader the tax base, the lower the tax rate necessary to raise a given amount of revenue.

Furthermore, the broader the VAT base, the more efficient it is. The exclusion of goods from taxation changes their prices relative to taxed goods. Changes in relative prices cause economic distortions. Consumers tend to substitute lower priced goods for higher priced goods.

There are three primary justifications for excluding specific items from taxation under a VAT.[10] First, the VAT would be difficult to collect because sellers of some types of goods and services could easily avoid reporting their sales. For example, VAT would be difficult to collect on expenditures for domestic services and expenditures abroad by U.S. residents. Second, some goods are excluded on equity grounds, since these goods claim disproportionately large percentages of the incomes of lower income families. (Data on spending patterns do not, however, suggest that exclusions can have a very powerful effect on the distribution of a VAT).[11] Third, some goods may be excluded because they are merit goods, that is "goods the provision of which society (as distinct from the preferences of the individual consumer) wishes to encourage..."[12] Some items may be justified for exclusion for more than one reason.

As shown in appendix D, broad and narrow bases for a VAT were formulated by CRS after reviewing the literature and examining practices of countries in the OECD. For fiscal year 1995, a broad–based VAT would tax 77.7 percent of total consumption and a narrow–based VAT would tax 46.5 percent.[13] OECD "data...suggest that...over 70 percent of total consumption was usually in the base of VAT countries."[14] For OECD nations, particularly those in the European Community (EC), there has been a trend towards

---

[10] This classification of justifications for exclusion from VAT taxation was derived from the following source: Tait, Alan A. *Value–Added Tax: International Practice and Problems*. Washington, International Monetary Fund, 1988. p. 56.
[11] U.S. Congressional Budget Office. *Effects of Adopting a Value–Added Tax*. Washington, U.S. Govt. Print. Off., February 1992, p. 22–26.
[12] Musgrave, Richard A., and Peggy B. Musgrave. *Public Finance in Theory and Practice*. 4th ed. New York, McGraw–Hill, 1984. p. 78.
[13] These CRS bases are remarkably close to the VAT bases formulated by Charles E. McLure, Jr., and Richard A. and Peggy B. Musgrave. For a comparison of these tax bases, see: *Value–Added Tax: Revenue Estimates for FY95*, p. 2–7.
[14] *Taxing Consumption*. Paris, Organization for Economic Cooperation and Development, 1988. p. 107.

broadening their VAT bases.[15] But OECD nations still exempt or zero–rate numerous goods.[16]

Revenue Estimates

If the VAT is a new revenue source, its gross revenue would be partially offset by reductions in revenues from personal income taxes, corporate income taxes, and social security taxes. Based on estimating conventions and tax calculations by the Congressional Budget Office (CBO), CRS chose to assume that the reduction in taxes on income offset 25 percent of the revenue of the new tax.[17] For fiscal year 1995, it is estimated that, for each 1–percent levied, a broad–based VAT would generate *net* revenue of $28.2 billion as a new revenue source. Also, for fiscal year 1995, a narrow–based VAT, for each 1–percent levied, would generate net revenue of $16.9 billion as a new revenue source. These revenue estimates should be considered as approximations. The actual revenue yields could vary depending on the complexity and structure of the VAT.

The VAT's high revenue yield at a low tax rate not only makes it a possible source for deficit reduction but also has generated concerns among some that VAT revenues may finance a larger public sector. This issue of VAT and the size of government is examined in a later section of this report.

ADMINISTRATIVE COST

The value–added tax would require the expansion of the U.S. Internal Revenue Service. But the high revenue yield from a VAT could cause administrative costs to be low measured as a percentage of revenue yield. Tax studies in Sweden, the United Kingdom, Portugal, and Australia found that administrative costs as a percentage of revenue were less for their broad–based consumption taxes than for their income taxes.[18] The OECD has concluded that "data…suggest from the experiences of a few countries

---

[15] Ibid., p. 36.
[16] For summary examples of VAT exclusions for 15 OECD nations, see appendix E.
[17] If the revenue from a VAT is used to *replace* revenue from a tax on income then the offset of 25 percent would decline, consequently, the net revenue for each 1–percent of VAT levied would be higher. For a discussion of this topic, see: *Value–Added Tax: Revenue Estimates for FY95*, p. 9.
[18] *Taxing Consumption*, p. 203.

that consumption tax revenues can be collected at a lower average cost than income taxes for a similar amount of revenue."[19] But, for the purposes of this report, the relevant comparison is between a VAT collected by the credit-invoice method and an increase in the individual income tax because the United States already has an administrative apparatus to collect the individual income tax. A VAT would have significant administrative costs because it is a new tax, while the administrative costs of an increase in the individual income tax would be minimal.

The administrative expense per dollar of VAT collected would vary with the degree of complexity of the VAT, the amount of revenue raised, the national attitude towards tax compliance, and the level of the small business exemption. Proposed VATs for deficit reduction usually are estimated to yield approximately $100 billion per fiscal year which would result in the spreading of administrative costs.

Many countries exempt small businesses from the VAT in order to eliminate compliance costs of small businesses and reduce administrative costs of government. There would, of course, be some loss in economic efficiency because the VAT would be less neutral.[20]

Table 1. Ratio of Staff to Taxpayers to Administer a VAT

Country	Year	Ratio of Staff to Taxpayers
France	1982	1:173
Ireland	1984	1.130
Italy	1978	1:726
Netherlands	1979	1:280
Portugal	1986	1:215
Sweden	1982	1:250
United Kingdom	1983	1:149

Source: Adapted by CRS from Tait, Alan A. *Value–Added Tax: International Practice and Problems*. Washington, International Monetary Fund, 1988. p. 250.

For tax year 1995, the General Accounting Office (GAO) projected the cost of administering a U.S. VAT would be $1.221 billion if the VAT has a single rate, a broad base, and an exemption for businesses with gross receipts of less than $100,000.[21] The exemption of $100,000 reduces the number of

---
[19] Ibid., p. 205.
[20] The concept of tax neutrality is explained in a subsequent section of this report.
[21] U.S. General Accounting Office. *Value–Added Tax: Administrative Costs Vary with Complexity and Number of Businesses*. Washington, May 1993. p. 63.

taxpayers from 24 to 9 million, cuts administrative costs by about 33 percent, but lowers VAT revenue by less than three percent.[22]

The General Accounting Office assumed that small businesses would have the option of registering, i.e. opting into the VAT system. GAO assumed that 15 percent of businesses with less than $25,000 in annual gross receipts and 30 percent of businesses with between $25,000 and $100,000 in annual gross receipts would register voluntarily.[23] If small businesses did not have this option, then the number of taxpayers would decline from 9.0 million to 5.4 million under the $100,000 threshold.[24]

The lower the proposed VAT rate, the smaller is the revenue loss for a given exemption threshold. For example, assume that a small business purchases no inputs from other firms, therefore, it would remit the maximum possible VAT on its gross receipts. If the VAT rate is 5 percent and the exemption threshold is $100,000 in gross receipts then the maximum possible VAT that would otherwise be remitted by a small business would be $5,000 (.15 × $100,000). But, if the VAT rate is 15 percent then the maximum possible VAT that would otherwise be remitted by a small business would be $15,000 (.15 × $100,000). Raising the exemption level, however, reduces administrative costs. Since there is a tradeoff between loss revenue and savings in administrative costs as the exemption level is raised, it can be argued that a lower VAT rate justifies a higher exemption threshold because the revenue loss would be smaller. The VAT rate usually proposed for the United States is only 5 percent. Consequently, it can be argued that a proposed U.S. VAT should have a higher exemption threshold than European VATs which have higher VAT rates.

But, if all businesses must register then there would be 24.4 million taxpayers in 1995.[25] Without any exemption for small businesses, GAO projected a VAT with a single rate and a broad base would cost $1.833 billion and require 30,577 staff years to administer for 1995.[26] Thus, GAO projected a staff to taxpayer ratio of 1 to 798 (30,577 to 24.4 million) without an exemption threshold. If there is an exemption threshold of $100,000, then approximately 20,364 staff years would be required to administer the VAT with 9 million taxpayers which would result in a

---

[22] Ibid., p. 3–4.
[23] Ibid., p. 102.
[24] Ibid., p. 62.
[25] Ibid., p. 38.
[26] Ibid.

projected staff to taxpayer of 1 to 442 (20,364 to 9 million).[27] Both of these staff to taxpayers ratios are much lower than the actual ratio of six out of seven listed nations in the EC shown in table 1. There may be some economies of scale in the administration of a VAT; furthermore, the VAT constructed by GAO for the United States is simpler and less costly to administer than existing VATs in the EC, so GAO's cost estimates could be fairly close to the mark. But a VAT may start out simple yet become extremely complex over time.

For fiscal year 1993, the U.S. Internal Revenue Service had operating costs of $7.08 billion and average positions realized of 113,352.[28] For fiscal year 1993, the IRS collected $1,176.7 billion; consequently, operating costs were 0.60 percent of revenue collected.[29] For fiscal year 1995, appropriations for the IRS totaled $7.49 billion.[30]

Table 2 lists administrative costs of value–added taxes for 12 nations in the OECD. It is difficult to compare administrative costs of a VAT among nations because of differences in tax complexity, quality of administration, standard rate of taxation, tax compliance, and data availability.[31]

COMPLIANCE

Nations in the OECD have experienced better compliance with their VATs than with either their individual or business income taxes. There are four reasons for this better compliance. First, a VAT collected using the credit–invoice method offers the opportunity to cross–check returns and invoices. For example, VAT shown on a sales invoice of a wholesaler will appear on the purchase invoice of a retailer. A tax auditor can examine both invoices to cross–check the accuracy of the tax returns of both the wholesaler and the retailer.

---

[27] CRS estimated the staff level of 20,364 by the following procedure. The ratio of $1.221 billion (GAO's estimated cost of a VAT with an exemption threshold of $100,000) to $1.833 billion (GAO's estimated cost of a VAT without an exemption threshold) equals .666. Multiplying 30,577 staff years (staff for a VAT without an exemption threshold) by .666 equals 20,364 staff years.

[28] U.S. Department of the Treasury. Internal Revenue Service. *Annual Report 1993*. Washington, U.S. Govt. Print. Off., 1995. [forthcoming]

[29] Ibid.

[30] Marrin, Rob and Vandana Mathurs. Status Quo Budget for IRS Proposes 9.8% Increase over 1995. *Daily Tax Report*, no. 25, February 7, 1995. p. G7.

Table 2. Administrative Costs of Value–Added Taxes

Country	Administrative Costs[a] (U.S. $)[b]	Administrative Costs Per Registered Trader (U.S. $)	Administrative Costs Per Staff Member (U.S. $)	Administrative Costs as a Percentage of Revenue[a]
Belgium	$101.7M[i]	$175	$25,686	1.09%
Denmark	57.2M	155	30,106	0.69
Finland	21.3M	235	43,599	0.41
France	224.2M[c]	n.a.	23,353	0.40
Ireland	21.0M	196	28,718	1.08
Italy	147.3M	105	24,544	0.49
Luxembourg	n.a.	n.a.	n.a.	0.99
New Zealand	10.5M[d]	46	10,490	0.49[e]
Norway	18.9M	67	31,531	0.32
Portugal	16.1M[f]	48	17,870[g]	1.00[f]
Sweden	31.1M[h]	68	37,914	0.35
United Kingdom	294.0M	200	30,175	0.95[j]

[a] 1985 unless otherwise indicated.
[b] At end of 31 December 1986.
[c] Does not include costs of customs authorities.
[d] 1987.
[e] Revenue is 1987-88 estimate taken from "1987 Budget" (NZ Govt. Printer, Wellington), administrative costs are for 1987.
[f] 1986; does not include costs of customs authorities.
[g] Does not include staff in local tax offices or in tax control services.
[h] 1988; does not include costs of customs authorities (est. $19.3M, 1982) costs of collecting the tax (est. $4.2M, 1982), or costs of the courts (est. $0.73M, 1982).
[i] 1986.
[j] Revenue is for 1985, administrative costs are for 1986.
Source: Adapted by CRS from *Taxing Consumption*. Paris, Organization for Economic Cooperation and Development, 1988. p. 204.

Second, each firm has an incentive not to allow suppliers to understate VAT on their sales invoices. A firm is able to credit VAT paid on inputs against VAT collected on sales; consequently, a firm's net VAT liability will increase if VAT shown on its purchase invoices was understated by suppliers.

---

[31] *Taxing Consumption*, p. 203, 205.

Third, tax auditors can compare information about a VAT with information about business income taxation which will increase compliance with both types of taxes. For example, the sales revenue figure reported on business income tax forms may be checked for consistency with gross VAT collected as shown on VAT forms. Also, a check of cash receipts during a VAT audit may identify the underreporting of sales. The firm may attempt not only to evade the VAT but also to evade the business income tax.[32] Having a single agency audit the VAT and business incomes taxes promotes efficiency in comparing tax information. Only three nations in the OECD have more than one tax agency.[33]

Fourth, some firms legally required to remit VAT may not register. But these firms receive no credit for VAT paid on inputs. Hence, these firms are only partially able to evade the VAT because of the compliance with the VAT by suppliers. This partial taxation of the underground economy by the VAT contrasts with the complete evasion of income taxation by underground firms.

Although compliance with a VAT is higher than the individual or business income tax, the level of compliance has been below initial expectations of tax authorities. As previously discussed, some firms legally required to remit VAT may not register.

Furthermore, firms may evade VAT by altering or omitting information as indicated in the following ten major types of evasion. First, a registered firm may not record resales of goods purchased from unregistered suppliers. Second, a seller of both exempt and taxable goods may divert purchased inputs on which VAT is claimed against taxed sales to help produce and sell exempt goods. Third, a firm may claim credit for purchases that are not creditable. For example, a firm's owner may claim credit for VAT paid on an automobile but then use it for nonbusiness purposes. Fourth, a firm may illegally import goods, charge VAT on their sale, but not report this VAT. Fifth, a firm may simply underreport sales which is the most common type of evasion. Retailers are the most frequent users of this type of evasion. Sixth, a firm may collect VAT on sales and then disappear. This type of evasion is particularly common to small firms in the construction industry. Seventh, in those nations with multiple rates, a firm may illegally reclassify goods into categories with lower tax rates. Eighth, the owners of some small firms, particularly retailers, may consume part of their firms' production but not record their consumption. Ninth, a firm may submit completely false

---

[32] *Taxing Consumption*, p. 199–200.
[33] Ibid., p. 201.

export claims in order to obtain illegal VAT refunds. Tenth, two firms may barter goods in order to evade the VAT.[34]

EQUITY

A major topic concerning any proposed tax or tax change is the distribution or equity of the tax among households. There are two types of equity: vertical and horizontal. Vertical equity concerns the tax treatment of households with different abilities–to–pay. Horizontal equity concerns the degree to which households with the same ability–to–pay are taxed equally. Both vertical and horizontal equity may be affected by the measure of ability–to–pay and the tax period.

Ability–to–Pay

The most common measure of ability–to–pay is income.[35] Proponents of income as a measure of ability–to–pay argue that saving yields utility by providing households with greater economic security. Federal data are more readily available on different measures of income than different levels of consumption. For example, the Federal Government reports levels of disposable income which equals consumption plus saving.[36] Thus, tax economists can more easily calculate tax incidence if income instead of consumption is the measure of ability-to-pay.

Some arguments for the consumption tax base suggest that personal consumption is the best measure of ability–to–pay because consumption is the actual taking of scarce resources from the economic system. Some

---

[34] For a detailed discussion of these ten types of evasion, see: Tait, Alan A. *Value–Added Tax: International Practice and Problems*. Washington, International Monetary Fund, 1988. p. 308–314.

[35] For an overview of the incidence of the VAT using income as a measure of ability–to–pay, see: CBO, *Effects of Adopting a Value–Added Tax*, p. 31–47.

[36] Economists generally prefer a theoretical concept of income called Haig–Simons income which equals consumption plus change in net worth. The Federal Government does not collect data on Haig–Simons income. The U.S. Treasury has used available data to approximate Haig–Simons income with a measure which the U.S. Treasury calls *economic income*. For a definition of economic income and an its use to measure the incidence of a VAT, see: Brashares, Edith, Janet Furman Speyrer, and George N. Carlson. Distributional Aspects of a Federal Value–Added Tax. *National Tax Journal*, v. 41, no. 2, June 1988. p. 158–159, 174.

economists argue that consumption may be a better proxy for permanent income than is current income (see discussion below).

Time Period

Tax incidence usually is measured by using a one–year period. Data on consumption and income are readily available in one–year increments and the concept of a one–year period is easily understood. But many economists believe tax incidence is more accurately determined by measuring consumption and income over a household's lifetime. Lifetime income and consumption are affected by the life cycle concept and transitional components of income. According to this life cycle concept, a household makes current consumption decisions based on its expected future flow of income, averaging its consumption over its lifetime.

For example, a common life cycle is low income in the household's early years, high income in the household's middle years, and low income in the household's retirement years. A young household may save a small percentage of its income in order to acquire consumer durables. In its middle years, this household may save a high percentage of its income while its income is highest. Finally, during its retirement years, this household may save a small percentage of its income in order to maintain its consumption level. Thus, annual consumption tends to be more stable than annual income over the household's life cycle.

Although many economists prefer the concept of lifetime income, Federal data are not collected on a lifetime basis. Consequently, economists have developed life–cycle models in an attempt to measure equity, but the distributional results from these models are subject to widespread debate.

Vertical Equity[37]

If disposable income over a one–year period is the measure of ability–to–pay then a VAT would be viewed as extremely regressive; that is, the percentage of disposable income paid in VAT would decrease rapidly as disposable income increases. In most discussions of tax policy, both a one–

---

[37] For a comprehensive analysis of the vertical equity of a VAT, see: Caspersen, Erik and Gilbert Metcalf. Is a Value–Added Tax Progressive? Annual Versus Lifetime Incidence Measures. *National Tax Journal*, v. 47, no. 4, December 1994. p. 731-746 and CBO, *Effects of Adopting a Value–Added Tax*, p. 31–47.

year period and annual disposable income (or some other annual income measure) are used; consequently, the VAT is viewed as being extremely regressive. For example, CBO calculated the annual incidence of a 3.5 percent broad-based VAT for 1992. CBO found that all families would have paid 2.2 percent of their income in VAT. The burden on family income was 4.8 percent on the lowest quintile, 3.2 percent on the second quintile, 2.8 percent on the middle quintile, 2.3 percent on the fourth quintile, and 1.5 percent on the highest quintile.[38]

If disposable income over a lifetime is the measure of ability-to-pay, a VAT would be mildly regressive. For lower and middle income households, it appears that nearly all savings are eventually consumed.[39] Thus, it may be that for the vast majority of households, lifetime consumption and lifetime income are approximately equal. High income households tend to have net savings over their lifetimes; consequently, they would pay a lower proportion of their disposable incomes in VAT than lower income groups.

If consumption is used as a measure of ability-to-pay, a single-rate VAT with a broad base would be approximately proportional regardless of the time period. In other words, the percentage of consumption paid in VAT by households would be approximately constant as the level of household consumption rises.

Another equity issue concerns the burden of a VAT on different age groups. If older individuals on the average consume more out of savings than younger individuals then a VAT would fall more heavily on the old than the young. Conversely, an increase in the personal income tax would fall more heavily on the young than the old.[40]

Policy Options to Alleviate Regressivity

Some supporters of progressive taxation oppose the VAT primarily because they believe that it is regressive. No mechanism is likely to introduce progressivity at higher income levels. But critics are especially concerned about the absolute burden of a VAT on low income households. The degree of regressivity on lower income households, however, can be

---

[38] CBO, *Effects of Adopting a Value-Added Tax*, p. 35.
[39] Modigliani estimates that at least 80 percent of all savings by households are eventually spent on consumption, see: Modigliani, Franco. The Role of Intergenerational Transfer and Life Cycle Saving in the Accumulation of Wealth. *Journal of Economic Perspectives*, v. 2, no. 2, Spring 1988. p. 15–23.
[40] For an analysis of intergenerational equity, see: Gravelle, Jane G. Assessing a Value-Added Tax: Efficiency and Equity. *Tax Notes*, v. 38, no. 10, March 7, 1988. p. 1,122–1,123.

reduced by Government policy. Three often-mentioned policies are exclusions and multiple rates, income tax credits, and earmarking of some revenues for increased social spending (including indexed transfer payments).

Exclusions and Multiple Rates

The incidence of the VAT depends on its tax base; therefore, the regressivity of the VAT can be reduced or eliminated by excluding (zero-rating or exempting) those goods that account for a disproportionately high percentage of the incomes of lower income households. The exclusion of many necessities on equity grounds from retail sales taxes has been politically popular at the State level. All members of the European Community exclude some goods from VAT on equity grounds. Also, except for Denmark and the United Kingdom, all EC nations have multiple tax rates on equity grounds. Reduced rates are applied to necessities and premium rates are levied on luxuries.

Despite the existing policies in the EC, most tax economists oppose exclusions and multiples rates to reduce regressivity for three reasons. First, the administrative costs, compliance costs, and neutrality costs are very high. If a VAT is to raise a given amount of revenue, then revenue lost from excluding goods must be offset by higher VAT rates. These higher rates increase the distortion in relative prices, and consequently, reduce the neutrality of the tax system. Second, the possible reduction in regressivity from exclusion and multiple rates is declining because consumption patterns for different income levels are becoming more similar.[41] Third, for a one-year time period, the reduction in regressivity is limited, particularly for low income households. Money saved for exclusions is largely offset by higher tax rates (needed for revenue neutrality) on taxed goods.[42]

In 1980, economists from six European nations discussed the experiences of their nations with the value-added tax at a conference sponsored by the Brookings Institution. These economists wrote papers about their nations' experiences with the VAT. After editing these papers, Henry J. Aaron, a Senior Fellow at Brookings, concluded that

European experience with the value-added tax proves that it is possible to convert a tax that in its simplest form is proportional with respect to consumption and regressive with respect to income into a tax that is progressive with respect to consumption and proportional or slightly

---

[41] Tait, *Value-Added Tax: International Practice and Problems*, p. 218.
[42] Brashares et al., *Distributional Aspects of a Federal Value-Added Tax*, p. 165.

progressive with respect to income. The use of different rates for different classes of goods and services and of zero–rating and exemptions is the mechanism for achieving this goal.

Participants at the conference agreed that the use of multiple rates and especially of exemptions complicates administration and compliance and distorts consumption in ways that are unlikely to promote economic efficiency. Most conference participants agreed that these disadvantages outweighed any gains from reduced regressivity. They held that distributional objectives should be sought with other instruments, notably income taxes and direct transfers.[43]

The Member States of the European Community have recognized the advantages of a single rate and a broad base for a VAT. Member States agreed to harmonize their VATs. Most Member States had numerous rates, consequently, they decided that a change to a single rate would be too drastic an adjustment. Therefore, the Member States agreed to a lower limit of 15 percent for the standard VAT rate and the abolition of all higher rates on luxury goods. In addition, the Member States may have one or two reduced rates of not less than five percent on such goods as food and medicines.[44] Also, in the OECD nations, there is a trend towards fewer rates and a broader base.[45]

Tax Credits

The Federal Government could allow either a flat tax credit or a credit that diminishes as income rises in order to overcome the regressivity of a VAT. This credit method could be operated in two different ways. First, an individual could apply the credit against his Federal income tax liability and thus lower his liability on a dollar–for–dollar basis. If the tax credit exceeded the individual's tax liability, he could apply for a refund of the excess credit. A taxpayer already due a tax refund could increase the size of his refund by the amount of the tax credit. A household not subject to income taxation could apply for a tax refund equal to the credit. An income tax credit that declines as income increases could reduce regressivity more sharply than a flat income tax credit.

Second, a stand–alone credit system could be established which would not require an eligible household to file an income tax return in order to

---

[43] Aaron, Henry J., ed. *The Value–Added Tax: Lessons from Europe.* Washington, The Brookings Institution, 1981. p. 8–9.
[44] Commission of the European Communities. *A Single Market for Goods.* Luxembourg, 1993. p. 8.
[45] *Taxing Consumption*, p. 36.

obtain a refund for VAT paid. An eligible household would have to submit a simple form in order to receive a refund. A stand–alone credit system may be more effective than the income tax credit in encouraging low income households to file for a refund, but administrative and compliance costs would be higher.

A study by Brashares, Speyrer, and Carlson concluded that

> ...a system of reimbursements to low income individuals and families for value–added tax paid targets the most needy groups with comprehensive relief from the tax without requiring high value–added rates. These reimbursements, when combined with the automatic indexation of transfers, almost completely relieve the burden on those in the lowest income category and may, in fact, overcompensate some families.[46]

But a Federal credit system would incur some administrative costs which would increase the total administrative costs of a VAT. Furthermore, households incur implicit taxes if their credits are phased out (or income tested transfers reduced).

An examination of sales tax credits at the State level may yield some implications for a credit against a Federal VAT. At the State level, many eligible poor people have not filed for their State income tax refunds resulting from the sales tax credit. At the Federal level, the refundable earned income tax credit is not claimed by many eligible poor.

At the State level, tax administrators generally prefer the income tax credit over exempting food from the retail sales tax.[47] But the general public may favor the food exemption over the income tax credit. As of November 1993, 26 out of 46 States with the sales tax exempted food.[48] Only seven States have an income tax credit for their sales taxes. These States are Hawaii, Idaho, Kansas, New Mexico, South Carolina, Vermont, and Wyoming.[49] In the early 1980s, Massachusetts and Nebraska canceled their credits against their sales taxes.[50]

Earmarking of VAT Revenues

A third option to reduce or eliminate regressivity is to earmark some of the revenue from a VAT to finance an increase in income tested transfers.

---

[46] Brashares et al., Distributional Aspects of a Federal Value–Added Tax, p. 172.
[47] Due, John F., and John L. Mikesell. *Sales Taxation: State and Local Structure and Administration.* Baltimore, Johns Hopkins University Press, 1983. p. 65.
[48] Advisory Commission on Intergovernmental Relations. *Significant Features of Fiscal Federalism: Budget Processes and Tax Systems.* Washington, June 1994. p. 96-97.
[49] Tait, *Value–Added Tax: International Practice and Problems,* p. 218.

Aaron estimates that an increase in benefits of approximately $5 billion for a VAT yielding $100 billion could fully protect low–income families from paying the VAT.[51]

For example, a 10–percent increase in food stamp entitlements would approximately offset the effect on households eligible for the full food stamp allotment of a VAT that raised $100 billion in revenue. This estimate is based on the fact that $100 billion will be approximately three percent of consumption in 1989 and that food is estimated to absorb about 30 percent of the budget in estimates of poverty thresholds.[52]

Most households with low taxable incomes do not currently receive transfers and would not be protected by Aaron's scheme.

Horizontal Equity

If disposable income is the measure of ability–to–pay, the horizontal equity of a VAT would depend on the time period. For a one–year period, a VAT would be very inequitable because households with the same level of disposable income would have widely differing levels of consumption, and, consequently, payments of VAT.

For a lifetime period, the VAT would have a high degree of horizontal equity. For low– and middle–income households, almost all income is consumed over these households' lifetimes; consequently, households with the same lifetime incomes would have the same levels of consumption and the same VAT payments.[53] Over their lifetimes, high income households with equal incomes differ in their levels of consumption, and, consequently, VAT payments. Thus, the VAT is not horizontally equitable for high income households.

If consumption is the measure of ability–to–pay, a single–rate VAT with a broad base would be horizontally equitable for either a one–year period or a lifetime period. Households with the same level of consumption would pay approximately the same VAT at all levels of consumption.

---

[50] Ibid.
[51] Aaron, Henry J. The Political Economy of a Value–Added Tax in the United States. *Tax Notes*, v. 38, no. 10, March 7, 1988. p. 1,113.
[52] Ibid.
[53] Aaron, Henry J. The Value–Added Tax: Sorting Through the Practical and Political Problems. *The Brookings Review*, Summer 1988. p. 13.

NEUTRALITY

In public finance, the more *neutral* is a tax, the less the tax affects private economic decisions; and, consequently, the more efficient is the operation of the economy. Conceptually, a VAT on all consumption expenditures with a single rate that is constant over time would be relatively neutral compared to other major revenue sources.

For households, two out of three major decisions would not be altered by this hypothetical VAT. First, this VAT would not alter choices among goods because all would be taxed at the same rate. Thus, *relative* prices would not change. In contrast, other taxes, such as excise taxes, which change relative prices, would distort household consumer choices by encouraging the substitution of untaxed goods for taxed goods. But a hypothetical income tax on all income would be neutral in this respect.

Second, a VAT does not affect the relative prices of present and future consumption. In contrast, the individual income tax affects the relative prices of present and future consumption because the income tax is levied on income which is saved, and then the returns on saving are taxed.

A household's work–leisure decision, however, would be affected by a VAT or any other tax on either consumption or income. Since leisure would not be taxed, any tax increase would fall on the returns to work.

A VAT would have conflicting effects on the number of hours worked by each household. A household would have an incentive to substitute leisure for work because of the relative rise in the value of leisure to work (substitution effect). Conversely, a household would have an incentive to increase its hours worked in an attempt to maintain its current living standards (income effect). Thus, a VAT could decrease, increase, or not change a household's hours worked.

For a firm, the VAT would not affect decisions concerning method of financing (debt or equity), choice among inputs (unless some suppliers are exempt or zero–rated), type of business organization (corporation, partnership, or sole proprietorship), and goods to produce. Other types of taxes may affect one or more of these types of decisions.

But a VAT cannot be levied on all consumer goods; consequently, prices of taxed goods will rise relative to untaxed goods. Furthermore, most nations with VATs have more than one rate.[54] Multiple VAT rates alter relative prices of taxed goods. Finally, VAT rates in most nations have tended to rise over time. Despite these deviations from a pure form of VAT,

---

[54] For a list of different VAT rates by country, see appendix F.

a broad–based VAT is relatively neutral compared to most other taxes. This neutrality is greater if the tax rate is relatively low. But the relative neutrality of a VAT compared to an increase in the personal income tax is uncertain.[55]

NATIONAL SAVING

National saving consists of government saving, business saving, and personal saving.[56] A VAT or any other tax that reduces the budget deficit would be expected to reduce government dissaving, and, consequently, raise national saving.[57]

A second issue concerns the effect on the personal savings rate of levying a VAT compared to increasing income taxes. A VAT would tax savings when they are spent on consumption, allowing savings to compound at a pre–tax rate. But an income tax is levied on all income at the time it is earned, regardless of whether the income is consumed or saved. The income tax is also levied on the earnings from income saved. Consequently, some proponents of the VAT have argued that choosing a VAT rather than an income tax to raise revenue would increase the return from saving, and, consequently, raise the savings rate.

The rate of return on savings, however, has never been shown to have a significant effect on the savings rate because of two conflicting effects. First, each dollar saved today results in the possibility of a higher amount of consumption in the future. This relative increase in the return from saving causes a household to want to substitute saving for consumption out of current income (substitution effect).

But a higher rate of return on savings raises a household's income; consequently, the household has to save less to accumulate some target amount of savings in the future (income effect). Thus, this income effect encourages households to have higher current consumption and lower current saving.

A CRS study compared the long-run effects on the capital stock and consumption of a $60 billion VAT and a $60 billion increase in individual income taxes. This study's results suggest that selecting a VAT instead of an

---

[55] See: CBO, *Effects of Adopting a Value–Added Tax*. p. 56–60 and Gravelle, Jane G. Income, Consumption, and Wage Taxation in a Life–Cycle Model: Separating Efficiency from Redistribution. *American Economic Review*, vol. 81, no. 4, September 1991: 985–995.

[56] For an explanation of the components of national saving, see: Rose, Harold. *The Question of Saving*. London, British–North American Committee, 1991. p. 1–3.

[57] For a comprehensive analysis of the U.S. saving rate, see: U.S. Congressional Budget Office. *Assessing the Decline in the National Saving Rate*. Washington, April 1993. 44 p.

increase in individual income taxes would raise the capital stock by less than two percent and consumption by only a quarter to a third of a percent after 50 years.[58]

An empirical study by the Congressional Budget Office analyzed the economic effects of replacing a quarter of the current income tax with a 6 percent VAT on all consumption. CBO estimated that this tax substitution would, in the long–run, increase the saving rate by 0.5 percent, raise the capital stock by 7.9 percent, increase output by 1.5 percent, and raise consumption by 1.2 percent.[59] These CBO findings of only slight economic effects in the long–run are consistent with the estimates of the CRS study.

INFLATION

If the Federal Reserve implemented an expansionary monetary policy to offset the contractionary effects of a VAT then there would be a one–time increase in the price level. For example, an expansionary monetary policy to accommodate a four percent VAT on 75 percent of consumer outlays might directly cause an estimated one–time increase in consumer prices of approximately three percent. There would also be some secondary price effects. Some goods would rise in price because their factors of production, especially labor, are linked to price indexes. Yet, if the Federal Reserve disregarded these secondary price increases in formulating monetary policy, these secondary price increases would tend to be offset by price reductions in other sectors of the economy.

An examination of VATs in the OECD have found only an initial effect of a VAT on the price level. But it is difficult to empirically isolate the effect of a VAT from other possible causes of a change in the price level.

It has been suggested that the Federal Government exclude the VAT from price indexes. Hence, existing indexing would not have an inflationary effect.[60] But this proposal could be unpopular and could be contested in court.

In summary, the proper monetary accommodation for a VAT would probably cause a one–time increase in the price level but not affect the

---
[58] U.S. Library of Congress. Congressional Research Service. *Economic Effects of a Value–Added Tax on Capital Formation*. Report No. 88–697 S, by Jane G. Gravelle. Washington, 1988. p. 2.
[59] CBO, *Effects of Adopting a Value–Added Tax*, p. 52–53.
[60] Aaron, The Political Economy of a Value–Added Tax in the United States, p. 1, 113.

subsequent rate of inflation, i.e., cause continual increases in the general price level.

BALANCE-OF-TRADE

Currently, all nations with VATs zero-rate exports and impose their VATs on imports. This procedure for taxing trade flows is referred to as the *destination principle* because a commodity is taxed at the location of consumption rather than production. An alternative would be to apply the *origin principle* by having all nations levy their VATs on exports but not imports.[61] All experts on the VAT recommend that nations adopting a VAT use the destination principle in order to be consistent with existing practices of other countries.

The destination principle creates a level playing field because imported commodities rise in price by the percentage of the VAT, but exported commodities do not increase in price. For a particular nation, the VAT rate on domestically produced and imported products would be the same. The VAT rate on a particular good would still vary among nations.

A simple example demonstrates this concept of a level playing field. Assume nation A has a 10 percent VAT and nation B has a 20 percent VAT. Exports from nation A to nation B would not be taxed by nation A. But nation B would levy a 20 percent VAT on imports from nation A. Thus, consumers in nation B would pay a 20 percent VAT regardless of whether their purchased goods were domestically produced or imported. Furthermore, exports from nation B to nation A would not be taxed by nation B. Nation A would levy a 10 percent VAT on imports. Hence, consumers in nation A would pay a 10 percent VAT on both domestically produced and imported commodities.

In 1962, the rules applicable to taxation were included in the General Agreement on Tariffs and Trade (GATT). Under these GATT rules, indirect taxes were rebatable on exports but direct taxes were not rebatable. Taxes which are not shifted but borne by the economic entity on which they are levied are classified as direct taxes. From 1962 through 1972, a fixed exchange rate system prevailed and the United States ran deficits in its

---

[61] Member States of the European Community (EC) have agreed, (beginning January 1, 1997), to apply the origin principle to sales within the EC but to continue to apply the destination principle to sales between a member state and an external nation. For an explanation of this change, see: Hart, Craig A. The European Community's Value-Added Tax System: Analysis

balance-of-payments. U.S. officials complained that the GATT rules favored nations with VATs because their exports were zero-rated. In contrast, corporate income taxes were not rebated on exports.

In early 1973, the United States and its major trading partners formally shifted to a flexible exchange rate system. Under this system, the supply and demand for different currencies determine their relative value. If a nation has a deficit in its balance-of-payments, its currency will tend to decline in value relative to the currencies of other nations. Thus, U.S. officials ended their complaints about the effects of GATT tax rules on international trade.

Since early 1973 there have been periods when exchange rates have been "managed" by mutual agreement among governments. Central banks have coordinated purchases and sales of different currencies in order to stabilize their relative values to promote international economic stability.

Even if there were a fixed exchange rate, a U.S. VAT would have slight impact on the balance-of-trade because the proposed VAT rate of 5 percent or less is a low tax rate. During the past six years the value of the dollar has fallen by over 40 percent relative to an index of major currencies, yet a serious U.S. balance-of-trade deficit persists. *In summary, a U.S. VAT offers no major advantage over other major tax increases in reducing the U.S. balance-of-trade deficit.*

Any large U.S. tax increase which reduces the Federal deficit could reduce the U.S. balance-of-trade deficit. The U.S. Treasury would reduce its borrowing on financial markets; interest rates would decline; and foreign capital would flow out of the United States. This capital outflow would reduce the demand for dollars relative to other currencies. This decline in the value of the dollar would raise exports, reduce imports, and, consequently, reduce the U.S. balance-of-trade deficit.

SIZE OF GOVERNMENT[62]

In the public policy debate over a VAT, one of the more divisive issues concerns the size of the public sector. There is widespread debate among economists and public policy experts concerning the variables that determine the size of government. These variables include urbanization, the growth of income, the age distribution of the population, technological change, relative

---

of the New Transitional Regime and Prospects for Further Harmonization. *International Tax and Business Lawyer*, v. 12, no. 1, 1994. p. 1-62.

[62] The optimal size of government is a value judgment. A larger public sector is neither inherently better nor worse than the existing size of the public sector.

costs of public services, social philosophy, rates of voter turnout, perceived need for defense spending, tax structure, and the size of a nation.[63]

It can be argued that a VAT is a "money machine" because the high revenue yield per one percent levied could allow the government to finance a growing public sector by periodically raising the VAT rate. Furthermore, it can be argued that the VAT is a partially "hidden" tax because consumers pay a small amount of VAT with each purchase and are not fully cognizant of the aggregate VAT paid for a year. Furthermore, the tax authorities can prohibit the VAT from being shown on retail sales slips.

But it can be argued that the tax rate for any tax can be increased at the margin. There is no proof that taxpayers are any less cognizant of a tax paid in small amounts than in one lump sum. Tax authorities can require that the VAT be shown on retail sales slips. Even if taxes are visible, it does not mean that they are superior in inducing voters to make the "right" choices, unless the benefits of taxes are similarly visible.

OECD nations with VATs have larger public sectors, on average, than nations without VATs, but this was also true before these nations approved their VATs. Some empirical studies have found that tax increases lead to increased spending, but other empirical studies have found that public demands for a larger public sector lead to tax increases. Hence, empirical studies are inconclusive concerning whether or not the passage of a VAT will increase the size of the public sector.

INTERGOVERNMENTAL ISSUES

Six of the 24 OECD nations including the United States, have federal systems of government. For the United States, a Federal VAT raises two primary intergovernmental issues: the Federal encroachment on the State sales tax and the joint collection of a VAT.[64]

---

[63] For a discussion of variables that may affect the size of government, see: Musgrave, Richard A., and Peggy B. Musgrave. *Public Finance in Theory and Practice*. 4th ed. New York, McGraw–Hill, 1985. p. 146–153.

[64] For an overview of State tax officials' concerns related to the enactment of a broad–based Federal consumption tax, see: U.S. General Accounting Office. *State Tax Officials Have Concerns About a Federal Consumption Tax*. Washington, March 1990. 77 p.

Encroachment on a State Tax Source

It has been claimed that broad–based consumption taxation has traditionally been a State source of revenue while income taxation has been a Federal revenue source; consequently, a Federal VAT would encroach on a primary source of tax revenue for the States.

But most States adopted their individual income taxes before they adopted their general sales taxes. Thirty–nine States levy both individual income taxes and general sales taxes. Twenty–three of these States adopted their individual income taxes in an earlier year than they adopted their general sales taxes. Three States adopted their individual income taxes and their general sales taxes in the same year. Thirteen States adopted their general sales taxes in an earlier year than they adopted their individual income taxes.[65]

No constitutional restriction prevents the Federal Government from levying a VAT. Precedents exist for the Federal Government to levy a new tax that many States already levy. For example, the Federal Government levied death taxes and personal income taxes after many States had already imposed them. Also, both the Federal Government and the States impose many of the same excise taxes.

The Federal Government relies primarily on income taxes (table 11 of appendix I), but taxation of income by States has risen steadily over the years (table H1 of appendix H). For fiscal year 1992 31.8 percent of State tax collections consisted of individual income taxes and 6.6 percent consisted of corporation income taxes. Total State taxes on income accounted for 38.4 percent of all taxes collected compared to only 32.8 percent collected from general sales taxation (including use taxes and gross receipts taxes). Hence, it can be argued that the States have encroached on the primary source of revenue of the Federal Government.

States could continue to levy their retail sales taxes while the Federal Government levies a VAT. The combined total of State (and local) sales taxes and a five percent VAT would be less than the standard VAT rate for most developed nations.[66] In Canada, the federal government levies a VAT, and the provinces continue to collect their retail sales taxes.

---

[65] For data on the dates of adoption of major State taxes by State, see appendix G.
[66] For data on sales tax rates by State, see appendix J.

Joint Collection

States could piggy–back on a Federal VAT. To do this, States would have to replace their retail sales taxes with a VAT and adopt the Federal tax base. Because a Federal VAT would probably have a broader base than any State sales tax, more revenue would be yielded for each one percent levied. Also, the broader VAT base would reduce economic distortions. A joint Federal–State VAT would eliminate duplication of administrative effort, permit the taxation of interstate mail order sales, and lower total compliance costs of firms.[67]

But, States may decline to do this because of their desire to maintain greater fiscal independence from the Federal Government. In 1962, Federal legislation permitted States to adopt the Federal individual income tax base and have the Federal Government collect its State income tax. No State has yet delegated collection of its income tax to the Federal Government.

In Canada, differences in tax bases for retail sales taxes in the provinces and the federal VAT have resulted in unexpectedly high administrative and compliance costs. Different tax bases have caused products to fall in four different tax categories: taxed by both political jurisdictions, taxed at the provincial level but not at the federal level, taxed at the federal level but not at the provincial level, and not taxed by either political jurisdiction. The federal government has tried to persuade the provinces to adopt the same tax base but they have refused.[68]

PUBLIC OPINION

Public opinion polls on a VAT for the United States have been limited. The public has been questioned, however, about a national sales tax (NST) and an increase in individual income taxes. A NST and a VAT are both broad–based consumption taxes with similar economic effects. The mass media sometimes refers to the VAT as a form of a NST. Hence, this section

---

[67] Alice M. Rivlin has proposed that the States assume full responsibility for most social services and that the Federal Government assist in financing this change through common shared taxes. One of her possible shared taxes would be a VAT. For her presentation of her proposal, see: Rivlin, Alice M. *Reviving the American Dream*. Washington, The Brookings Institution, 1992. 196 p.

[68] Rushton, Michael. A Value-Added Tax for the United States: Lessons from Canadian Experience. *National Tax Association–Proceedings of the Eighty-Sixth Annual Conference*, 1993. p. 98.

of the report assumes that public opinion towards a VAT would be similar to public opinion towards a NST.

Three opinion polls were selected for discussion in this report. First, a poll conducted for the Advisory Commission on Intergovernmental Relations (ACIR) has a detailed breakdown by demographic characteristics and individuals were asked to *choose between* an increase in individual income taxes and a NST on all purchases other than food. The two other polls, a Media General/Associated Press Poll and a Harris Poll, were selected because they are more current and were conducted by different polling organizations.

Data from these surveys are shown in appendix K. These data suggest a public preference for a VAT over an increase in individual income taxes. Demographic characteristics have only a slight influence on this preference.

APPENDIX A. CREDIT–INVOICE, SUBTRACTION, AND ADDITION METHODS

This appendix shows numerical examples of the three methods of calculating a VAT: credit–invoice, subtraction, and addition methods. The tax rate for a VAT may be *price inclusive* (included in the sales price) or *price exclusive* (added to the sales price). Currently all developed nations except Finland and Sweden levy their VAT rates on a price exclusive basis.[69]

The *credit–invoice method* of calculating a VAT is demonstrated in table A1. The rate for the value–added tax is assumed to be 10 percent on a price–exclusive basis. The product manufactured and sold is a widget. The production of widgets involves firms at four different stages of production: raw material producer, manufacturer, wholesaler, and retailer. The operating assumption is that the VAT is fully shifted forward to the next stage of production; consequently, the consumer pays the entire VAT. The seller indicates the amount of VAT on each sales invoice.

At the first stage of production, the simplifying assumption is made that the raw material producer provides all of his own inputs. The raw material producer has sales of $200 plus VAT on sales of $20 (10 percent of $200). Sales plus VAT equal $220 ($200 + $20). Because the raw material producer purchased no inputs, he receives no credit for prior VAT paid. Hence, the raw material producer remits $20 to the government.

---

[69] Tait, *Value–Added Tax: International Practice and Problems*, p. 8.

At the second stage of production, the manufacturer has sales of $500 plus VAT on sales of $50 (10 percent of $500) which is shown separately on the sales invoice. Sales plus VAT equal $550 ($500 + $50). The manufacturer purchased $200 in raw material plus $20 was paid in VAT as listed on the purchase invoice. The manufacturer credits the $20 paid in VAT on inputs against the $50 in VAT collected on sales and remits the difference of $30 to the government.

At the third stage of production, the wholesaler has sales of $750 and adds a VAT of $75 (10 percent of $750). Sales plus VAT equal $825 ($750 + $75). The wholesaler purchased inputs for $500 and paid an additional $50 in VAT. Consequently, the wholesaler credits $50 in VAT paid on inputs against $75 in VAT collected on sales and remits $25 in VAT to the government.

Finally, the retailer has sales of $1,000 and adds VAT of $100 (10 percent of $1,000). Sales plus VAT equal $1,100 ($1,000 + $100). The retailer purchased $750 in inputs and paid an additional $75 in VAT. The retailer credits the $75 in VAT paid on inputs against the $100 in VAT collected on sales and remits $25 to the government.

The VAT remitted by the four firms was $100. The consumer paid $100 in VAT on top of $1,000 in retail sales. The last line of figures in table A1 indicates the value added at each stage of production. The sum of all firms' value added is $1,000, which equals the sales price of the exclusive of VAT.

Table A1. Credit-Invoice Method (Data in U.S. dollars, price-exclusive VAT rate assumed at 10 percent)

Transaction	Stage of Production of Widgets				Total VAT Remitted
	Raw Material Producer[a]	Manufacturer	Wholesaler	Retailer	
Sales (Excluding VAT)	$200	$500	$750	$1,000	
VAT on Sales	20	50	75	100	
Purchases of Inputs (Excluding VAT)	0	200	500	750	
VAT on Inputs	0	20	50	75	
Credit, VAT on Inputs	-0	-20	-50	-75	
VAT to be Remitted	20	30	25	25	100
Value Added	200	300	250	250	

[a] As a simplification, the raw material producer is assumed to provide all of its inputs.

The *subtraction method* is demonstrated in table A2. In order to simplify a comparison with figures in table A1, a tax inclusive VAT rate of 9.091 percent is assumed. This tax inclusive rate is equivalent to a tax exclusive rate of 10 percent.

Table A2. Subtraction Method (Data in U.S. dollars, price-inclusive VAT rate assumed at 9.091 percent)

Transaction	Stage of Production of Widgets				Total VAT Remitted
	Raw Material Producer[a]	Manufacturer	Wholesaler	Retailer	
Sales (Including VAT)	$220	$550	$825	$1,100	
Purchases (Including VAT)	0	220	550	825	
VAT Base	220	330	275	275	
VAT to be Remitted	20	30	25	25	100

[a] As a simplification, the raw material producer is assumed to provide all of its inputs.

The raw material producer has sales including VAT of $220. Because it has no purchases of inputs, its VAT base (sales including VAT less purchases of inputs) is $220. Its VAT to be remitted is $20 (9.091 percent of $220).

The manufacturer has sales including VAT of $550 and purchases including VAT of $220. Its VAT base is $330 ($550 less $220). Its VAT to be remitted is $30 (9.091 percent of $330).

The wholesaler has sales including VAT of $825 and purchases including VAT of $550. Its VAT base is $275 ($825 less $550). Its VAT to be remitted is $25 (9.091 percent of $275).

Lastly, the retailer has sales including VAT of $1,100, purchases including VAT of $825, and its VAT base is $275 ($1,100 less $825). It remits VAT of $25 (9.091 percent of $275). The total VAT remitted to the government by all four firms is $100 ($20 + $30 + $25 + $25). This $100 in VAT equals 9.091 percent of $1,100.

The *addition method* is shown in table A3. The raw material producer calculates its value added by adding all payments for factors of production which the firm owned and applied to the production process. Thus, the raw material producer had value added of $200 (wages of $100, rent of $50, interest of $30, and profit of $20). Next, the raw material producer calculates VAT by multiplying its value added by the tax rate. Thus, the raw material producer must remit $20 ($200 × 0.1) to the Government. This procedure applies to all other stages of production and total VAT remitted is $100.

Table A3. Addition Method (Data in U.S. dollars, VAT rate assumed at 10 percent)

Return on Factors of VAT Production Remitted	Raw Material Producer[a]	Manufacturer	Wholesaler	Retailer	Total
Wages	$100	$150	$110	$80	
Rent	50	100	90	115	
Interest	30	25	35	30	
Profit	20	25	15	25	
Value added	200	300	250	250	
Value-added Tax	20	30	25	25	100

[a] As a simplification, the raw material producer is assumed to provide all of his inputs.

APPENDIX B. ECONOMIC EFFECTS OF A SPECIAL VAT TREATMENT

Table B1. Economic Effects of a Special VAT Treatment

Special VAT Treatment	Break in Chain of VAT Credits	Price of Commodity Plus VAT	Total VAT Remitted
Exempt Retailer	No	Decline Equal to a Fraction of Initial VAT	Decline
Zero-rated Retailer	No	Decline Equal to Eliminated VAT	Decline (VAT Eliminated)
Exempt Manufacturer	Yes	Rise	Rise
Zero-rated Manufacturer	Yes	No Change	No Change

Source: Revised excerpt from table 1 in U.S. Library of Congress. Congressional Research Service. *Economic Effects of a VAT on Small Business.* Report No. 88-288 E, by James M. Bickley. Washington, 1988. p. 7.

APPENDIX C. COMPOSITION OF TAXES

Table C1. Percentage Distribution of Tax Revenues in Selected Countries by Source, Total of All Levels of Government Fiscal Year 1990

	All Taxes	Taxes on Income and Profits[a]		Social Security Taxes			Taxes on Goods and Services			Property Taxes[d]	Other and Unallocable[e]
		Individual Income	Corporate Profits	Total[b]	Employers' Share	Employees' Share	Total[c]	General	Specific		
Australia	100.00%	43.2%	13.9%	—	—	—	27.8%	8.1%	15.2%	8.9%	6.1%
Austria	100.00	21.2	3.3	32.9%	16.2%	13.9%	31.5	20.8	9.0	2.7	7.3
Belgium	100.00	30.7	6.4	34.7	20.7	11.6	25.3	16.1	7.4	2.6	—
Canada	100.00	40.8	8.8	14.2	9.7	4.3	27.4	13.9	9.9	9.0	1.2
Denmark	100.00	52.7	3.3	3.1	0.7	2.4	33.4	20.5	11.0	4.2	0.8
Finland	100.00	46.8	5.5	7.4	7.4	—	37.3	24.1	12.7	2.8	0.2
France	100.00	11.8	5.4	44.2	27.3	13.3	28.2	18.8	8.5	5.2	5.2
Germany	100.00	27.4	4.7	36.8	18.8	15.9	27.4	17.0	9.4	3.3	0.4
Greece	100.00	14.5	5.6	28.4	12.8	13.4	45.7	27.2	16.0	4.8	0.7
Ireland	100.00	31.9	5.0	14.8	9.0	5.2	42.3	20.6	20.1	4.7	1.3
Italy	100.00	26.3	10.0	32.9	23.6	6.3	28.0	14.7	10.6	2.3	0.3
Japan	100.00	26.8	21.5	29.2	15.2	10.9	13.2	4.2	7.3	9.0	0.2
Luxembourg	100.00	24.1	18.2	27.7	13.5	10.7	23.5	13.9	9.1	8.5	—

	All Taxes	Taxes on Income and Profits[a]		Social Security Taxes			Taxes on Goods and Services			Property Taxes[d]	Other and Unallocable[e]
		Individual Income	Corporate Profits	Total[b]	Employers' Share	Employees' Share	Total[c]	General	Specific		
Netherlands	100.00	24.7	7.6	37.3	7.9	23.5	26.4	16.5	7.5	3.7	0.3
New Zealand[f]	100.00	46.5	6.5	—	—	—	33.7	22.6	9.2	8.2	1.8
Norway	100.00	25.9	8.9	26.2	16.6	8.4	35.4	18.3	15.6	2.9	0.9
Portugal	100.00	16.0	7.4	27.6	16.4	10.2	44.0	19.6	23.4	2.4	0.6
Spain	100.00	21.8	8.8	35.4	25.5	5.8	28.3	16.1	10.4	5.5	—
Sweden	100.00	37.9	3.1	27.6	25.4	—	24.6	14.6	9.0	3.5	3.4
Switzerland	100.00	34.6	6.5	32.8	10.3	10.4	18.3	10.0	7.1	7.8	—
Turkey	100.00	26.8	8.7	19.7	11.0	7.4	27.9	20.1	7.3	2.3	16.7
United Kingdom	100.00	28.4	11.0	17.5	10.0	6.6	30.4	16.8	12.3	8.4	4.3
United States	100.00	35.8	7.3	29.5	16.6	11.6	16.5	7.6	6.8	10.8	—

[a] Includes taxes on capital gains.
[b] Includes taxes on self-employed.
[c] Includes import duties, profits on public fiscal monopolies, licenses, and other business taxes.
[d] Includes taxes on movable and immovable property, net wealth taxes, and estate and gift taxes.
[e] Includes general and selective taxes on payrolls which are not earmarked for social security purposes, and other taxes not elsewhere classified.
[f] The central government accounting year has been changed such that the figures for the 1988 year show revenue for 12 months to March 1988. The figures for 1989 show revenue for the 12 months to June 1990.

Source: Tax Foundation, Inc. *Facts and Figures on Government Finance*. Washington, 1993. p. 36.

APPENDIX D. POSSIBLE BASES FOR A VALUE–ADDED TAX

Table D1. Possible Bases for a Value–Added Tax, 1993 (billions of U.S. dollars)

Total consumer expenditures		$4,378.2
Expenditures excluded from a broad–based VAT:		
Food furnished employees (including military)		12.0
Food produced and consumed on farms		0.4
Standard clothing issued to military personnel		0.3
Housing:		
Rental value of housing	629.0	
less: expenditures for new housing	218.3	
		410.7
Domestic service		11.5
Health insurance		46.2
Service furnished without payment by financial intermediaries[a]		146.2
Expense of handling life insurance		72.6
Net purchases of used autos		45.9
Auto insurance premiums less claims paid		27.5
Private education and research		105.5
Religious and welfare activities		123.0
Foreign travel and other, net		
Foreign travel by U.S. residents	40.8	
plus: expenditures abroad by U.S. residents	3.2	
less: expenditures in the U.S. by nonresidents	68.5	
less: personal remittances in kind to nonresidents	0.8	
		-25.3
Total exclusions		976.5
Broad VAT base		3,401.7
As percentage of total consumption		77.7%
Additional expenditures excluded from a narrow VAT base:		
Food purchased for off–premise consumption		422.2
Expenditures for new housing		218.3
Medical care (other than health insurance)		714.3

Clubs and fraternal organizations except insurance	9.5
Total additional exclusions	1,364.3
Narrow VAT base	2,037.4
As percentage of total consumption	46.5%

[a] Except life insurance carriers and private uninsured pension plans.
Source: Bases formulated by CRS using data from: U.S. Department of Commerce. *Survey of Current Business*, July 1994. Washington, 1994. p. 64, 83.

APPENDIX E. SUMMARY EXAMPLES OF EXEMPTIONS AND ZERO RATES

Table E1. VAT: Summary[a] Examples of Exemptions and Zero Rates

	BE	DK	FR	D	E	I	LU	N	NO	PO	ES	SE	TU	UK
Food: basic					Z	Z				Z				Z
Food: processed					Z									Z
Medical services		X	X	X	X	X	X	X	X	X	X	X	X	X
Medical drugs					Z					X		Z		Z
Educational services		X	X	X	X	X	X	X	X	X	X	X	X	X
Housing purchased														Z
Housing rented		X	X	X	X	X	X	X	X	X	X	X	X	X
Clothing					Z									
Books										Z				Z
Newspapers		Z						Z		Z		Z		Z
Entertainment, sports			X	X	X					X			X	
Museums		X		X						X	X			
Government sales of goods and services					X									
Financial services		X	X	X	X	X	X	X	X	X	X	X	X	X
Secondhand goods			X											
Agricultural inputs					Z					Z	X	X		
Original art		X	X							X	X	X		

Note: X = exemptions; Z = zero rate.

[a] The symbols are only summaries; for instance, Ireland does not zero rate all clothing, but only children's clothing and shoes.

BE = Belgium   N = Netherlands   I = Italy   TU = Turkey
DK = Denmark   NO = Norway   E = Ireland   SE = Sweden
FR = France   PO = Portugal   LU = Luxembourg   UK = United Kingdom
D = West Germany   ES = Spain

Source: Adapted by CRS from Tait, Alan A. *Value-Added Tax: International Practice and Problems*. Washington, International Monetary Fund, 1988, p. 52.7

APPENDIX F. VAT RATES BY COUNTRY

Table F1. Countries Adopting VAT and Percentage Rates Throughout the World[a]

Country	Date VAT Introduced or Proposed	At Introduction	November 1994
Algeria	Apr. 1992	7, 13, 21, 40	7, 13, 21, 40
Argentina	Jan. 1975	16	18, 26, 27[b]
Armenia	Jan. 1992	28	20
Austria	Jan. 1973	8, 16	10, 20, 32
Azerbaijan	Jan. 1992	28	20
Bangladesh	July 1991	15	15
Belarus	Jan. 1992	28	25
Belgium	Jan. 1971	6, 14, 18	1, 6, 12, 20.5
Benin	May 1991	18	18
Bolivia	Oct. 1973	5, 10, 15	14.92[f]
Brazil[c]	Jan. 1967	15	9, 11
Brazil[d]	Jan. 1967	15	17
Bulgaria	Apr. 1994	18	18
Burkina Faso	Jan. 1993	10, 15	15
Canada	Jan. 1991	7	7
Chile	Mar. 1975	8, 20	18
China	Jan. 1994	13, 17	13, 17
Colombia	Jan. 1975	4, 6, 10	8, 14, 20, 35, 45
Costa Rica	Jan. 1975	10	8
Côte d'Ivoire	Jan. 1960	8	5, 11, 20
Cyprus	July 1992	5	8[b]
Czech Republic	Jan. 1993	5, 23	5, 23
Denmark	Jul. 1967	10	25
Dominican Republic	Jan. 1983	6	6
Ecuador	Jul. 1970	4, 10	10
El Salvador	Sep. 1992	10	10
Estonia	Jan. 1992	10	18
Fiji	Jul. 1992	10	10
Finland	June 1994	22	9,12,22

Country	Date VAT Introduced or Proposed	At Introduction	November 1994
France	Jan. 1968	6.4, 13.6, 20, 25	2.1, 5.5, 18.6
Gabon	Mar. 1995	18	
Georgia	Mar. 1992	28	14
Ghana	Jan. 1995		
Germany	Jan. 1968	5, 10	7, 15
Grenada	Jan. 1987	30	5, 27.5
Greece	Jan. 1987	6, 18, 36	4, 8, 18
Guatemala	Aug. 1983	7	7
Haiti	Nov. 1982	7	10
Honduras	Jan. 1976	3	7, 10
Hungary	Jan. 1988	15, 25	10, 25
Iceland[g]	Jan. 1990	14, 24.5	14, 24.5
Indonesia	Apr. 1985	10	10, 20, 35
Ireland	Nov. 1972	5.26, 16.37, 30.26	12.5, 21
Israel	Jul. 1976	8	6.5, 17
Italy	Jan. 1973	6, 12, 18	4, 9, 12, 19
Jamaica	Oct. 1991	10	12.5
Japan[h]	Apr. 1989	3, 6	3, 4.5
Kazakhstan	Jan. 1992	28	13, 20
Kenya	Jan. 1990	17, 20, 40, 50, 270	5, 18, 40
Korea	Jul. 1977	10	2, 3.5, 10
Kyrghystan	Jan. 1992	28	20
Latvia[i]	Jan. 1992	10, 12, 14	18
Lithuania	May 1994	18	18
Luxembourg	Jan. 1970	2, 4, 8	3, 6, 12, 15
Madagascar	Jan. 1969	6, 12	15
Malawi	May 1989	10, 35, 55, 85	10, 20, 40
Mali	Jan. 1991	10, 17	10, 17
Malta	Jan. 1996	15	
Mexico	Jan. 1980	10	10
Moldova	Jan. 1992	28	14, 15, 20
Mongolia	May 1993	10	10
Morocco	Apr. 1986	7, 12, 14, 19,	7, 14, 19

Value-Added Tax: Concepts, Policy Issues, and OECD Experiences 43

Country	Date VAT Introduced or Proposed	At Introduction	November 1994
		30	
Netherlands	Jan. 1969	4, 12	6, 17.5
New Zealand	May 1986	10	12.5
Nicaragua	Jan. 1975	6	5, 6, 10
Niger	Jan. 1986	8, 12, 18	17
Norway	Jan. 1970	20	22
Pakistan	Nov. 1990	12.5	15
Panama	Mar. 1977	5	5, 10
Paraguay	Jul. 1993	12	10
Peru	Jul. 1976	3, 20, 40	18
Philippines	Jan. 1988	10	10
Poland	Jul. 1993	7, 22	7, 22
Portugal	Jan. 1986	8, 16, 30	5, 16, 30[k]
Romania	Jul. 1993	18	18
Russia	Jan. 1992	28	10, 20
Senegal	Mar. 1961–80[l]	...	7, 20, 30
Singapore	Apr. 1994	3	
Slovakia	Jan. 1993	5, 23	6, 25
South Africa	Sep. 1991	10	14
Spain	Jan. 1986	6, 12, 33	3, 6, 15
Sri Lanka	Apr. 1995	5, 20	
Sweden[g]	Jan. 1969	2.04, 6.38, 11.1	12[m], 21, 25
Switzerland	Jan. 1995	2, 6.5	
Taiwan	Apr. 1986	5	5, 15, 25
Tajikistan	Jan. 1992	28	20
Tanzania	mid. 1994		
Thailand	Jan. 1992	7	7
Trinidad and Tobago	Jan. 1990	15	15
Tunisia	Jul. 1988	6, 17, 29	6, 17, 29
Turkey	Jan. 1985	10	1, 8, 15, 23
Turkmenistan	Jan. 1992	28	20
Ukraine	Jan. 1992	22, 28	28
United Kingdom	Apr. 1973	10	17.5

Country	Date VAT Introduced or Proposed	At Introduction	November 1994
Uruguay	Jan. 1968	5, 14	12, 22
Uzbekistan	Jan. 1992	30	20
Western Samoa	Jan. 1994	10	10
Venezuela	Oct. 1993	10	10
Zambia	Jul. 1995^n		

[a] Rates shown in bold type are so-called effective standard rates (tax exclusive) applied to goods and services not covered by other especially high or low rates. Most countries use a zero-rate for a few goods, and Ireland and the United Kingdom use it extensively to ensure that substantial amounts of goods and services are free of VAT.

[b] Supplementary VAT rates of 8 and 9 percent on noncapital goods imports: through "catch-up," these can revert to 18 percent retail.

[c] On interstate transactions depending on region.

[d] On intrastate transactions.

[f] Effective rate (legislated tax inclusive rate is 13 percent.)

[g] Effective rates.

[h] An accounts-based (substantive) VAT; applies only to cars.

[i] Originally 10 percent on manufacturing and wholesale, 12 percent at retail, and 14 percent at health resorts.

[k] In the Azores and Madeira the rates are 4, 12, 21, respectively.

[l] Senegal's VAT evolved from a limited manufacturers' turnover tax with credits, and no precise date of introduction is given.

[m] A "tourist VAT rate" on hotel rooms, camping and domestic travel.

[n] Discussed

Source: Tait, Alan A. International Monetary Fund. Washington, November 18, 1994.

APPENDIX G. DATES OF ADOPTION OF MAJOR STATE TAXES BY STATE

Table G1. Dates of Adoption of Major State Taxes by State

State	Individual Income	Corporate Income	General Sales	Gasoline	Cigarettes	Distilled Spirits[a]
Alabama	1933	1933	1936	1923	1935	–
Alaska		1949	–	1946	1949	1959
Arizona	1933	1933	1933	1921	1935	1933
Arkansas	1929	1929	1935	1921	1929	1935
California	1935	1929	1933	1923	1959	1935
Colorado	1937	1937	1935	1919	1964	1933
Connecticut	1991[c]	1915	1947	1921	1935	1937
Delaware	1917	1957	–	1923	1943	1933
Florida	–	1971	1949	1921	1943	1935
Georgia	1929	1929	1951	1921	1937	1937
Hawaii	1901	1901	1935	1932	1939	1939
Idaho	1931	1931	1965	1923	1945	–
Illinois	1969	1969	1933	1927	1941	1934
Indiana	1963	1963	1933	1923	1947	1933
Iowa	1934	1934	1933	1925	1921	–
Kansas	1933	1933	1937	1925	1927	1948
Kentucky	1936	1936	1960	1920	1936	1934
Louisiana	1934	1934	1938	1921	1932	1934
Maine	1969	1969	1951	1923	1941	–

State	Individual Income	Corporate Income	General Sales	Gasoline	Cigarettes	Distilled Spirits[a]
Maryland	1937	1937	1947	1922	1958	1933
Massachusetts	1916	1919	1966	1929	1939	1933
Michigan	1967	1967	1933	1925	1947	–
Minnesota	1933	1933	1967	1925	1947	1934
Mississippi	1912	1921	1930	1922	1932	1966
Missouri	1917	1917	1934	1925	1955	1934
Montana	1933	1917	–	1921	1947	–
Nebraska	1967	1967	1967	1925	1947	1935
Nevada	–	–	1955	1923	1947	1935
New Hampshire	1923[b]	1970	–	1923	1939	–
New Jersey	1976	1958	1966	1927	1948	1933
New Mexico	1933	1933	1933	1919	1943	1934
New York	1919	1917	1965	1929	1939	1933
North Carolina	1921	1921	1933	1921	1969	–
North Dakota	1919	1919	1935	1919	1927	1936
Ohio	1971	1971	1934	1925	1931	–
Oklahoma	1915	1931	1933	1923	1933	1959
Oregon	1930	1929	–	1919	1965	–
Pennsylvania	1971	1935	1953	1921	1937	–
Rhode Island	1971	1947	1947	1925	1939	1933
South Carolina	1922	1922	1951	1922	1923	1935
South Dakota	–	–	1933	1922	1923	1935
	1931[b]	1923	1947	1923	1925	1939

State	Individual Income	Corporate Income	General Sales	Gasoline	Cigarettes	Distilled Spirits[a]
Texas	–	–	1961	1923	1931	1935
Utah	1931	1931	1933	1923	1923	–
Vermont	1931	1931	1969	1923	1937	–
Virginia	1916	1915	1966	1923	1960	–
Washington	–	–	1933	1921	1935	–
West Virginia	1961	1967	1933	1923	1947	–
Wisconsin	1911	1911	1961	1925	1939	1934
Wyoming	–	–	1935	1923	1951	–

[a]Excludes excises by the States that own and operate liquor stores, and by North Carolina where county stores operate under State supervision.
[b]Taxes are limited: New Hampshire and Tennessee (interest and dividends).
[c]Individual income tax imposed October 1, 1991. Prior to that date, tax was imposed on capital gains and dividends.
Source: Tax Foundation. *Facts and Figures on Government Finance.* Washington, 1994. p. 194.

Appendix H. Percentage Distribution of State Tax Collections by Source Selected Fiscal Years, 1902-1992

Year	Total	Individual Income	Corporate Income	General Sales, Use or Gross Receipts	Motor Fuels	Tobacco	Alcohol Sales and Licenses	Motor Vehicle and Operators' Licenses	Property	Death and Gift	Severance	Other
1902	100.0%	–	–	–	–	–	–	–	52.6%	–	–	47.4%
1913	100.0	–	–	–	–	–	0.7	1.7	46.5	–	–	51.2
1922	100.0	4.5	6.1	–	1.4	–	–	16.1	36.7	7.0	–	28.2
1927	100.0	4.4	5.7	–	16.1	–	–	18.7	23.0	6.6	–	25.5
1932	100.0	3.9	4.2	0.4	27.9	1.0	0.1	17.7	17.4	4.7	1.0	18.7
1934	100.0	4.0	2.5	8.7	28.5	1.3	4.1	15.4	13.8	4.5	1.1	15.9
1936	100.0	5.8	4.3	13.9	26.2	1.7	6.3	13.8	8.7	4.5	1.3	13.4
1938	100.0	7.0	5.3	14.3	24.8	1.8	7.2	11.5	7.8	3.4	1.9	14.0
1940	100.0	6.2	4.7	15.1	25.3	2.9	7.7	11.7	7.8	3.3	1.6	13.6
1941	100.0	6.2	5.5	15.9	25.3	2.9	7.5	12.0	7.4	2.8	1.5	12.3
1942	100.0	6.4	6.9	16.2	24.1	3.3	8.0	11.0	6.8	2.7	1.6	12.9
1943	100.0	7.4	8.6	16.9	19.6	3.6	8.5	10.4	6.5	2.7	1.9	13.9
1944	100.0	7.8	11.0	17.7	16.8	3.9	8.0	9.7	6.0	3.1	1.7	14.8
1945	100.0	8.2	10.4	17.8	17.9	3.3	8.5	9.7	6.3	2.9	1.9	14.8
1946	100.0	7.9	9.0	18.2	19.4	4.0	9.5	8.9	5.0	2.9	1.8	14.9
1947	100.0	7.3	7.9	20.6	18.7	4.3	8.4	9.0	4.6	2.7	1.6	14.0
1948	100.0	7.4	8.7	21.9	18.5	5.0	7.4	8.8	4.1	2.4	1.9	13.5
1949	100.0	8.0	8.7	21.8	19.5	5.3	6.8	9.0	3.7	2.1	2.7	13.1
1950	100.0	9.1	7.4	21.1	19.1	5.2	6.3	9.5	3.9	2.2	2.7	13.3
1951	100.0	9.0	7.7	22.4	19.0	4.8	6.1	9.4	3.9	2.1	2.5	12.9
1952	100.0	9.3	8.5	22.6	19.1	4.6	5.3	9.4	3.8	2.1	2.8	12.8

Year	Total	Individual Income	Corporate Income	General Sales, Use or Gross Receipts	Motor Fuels	Tobacco	Alcohol Sales and Licenses	Motor Vehicle and Operators' Licenses	Property	Death and Gift	Severance	Other
1953	100.0	9.1	7.7	23.1	19.0	4.4	5.2	9.6	3.5	2.1	2.7	13.5
1954	100.0	9.1	7.0	22.9	19.1	4.2	4.9	9.9	3.5	2.2	2.8	13.5
1955	100.0	9.4	6.4	22.7	20.0	4.0	4.7	10.2	3.6	2.1	2.6	13.9
1956	100.0	10.3	6.7	22.7	20.3	3.9	4.7	9.7	3.5	2.3	2.7	13.6
1957	100.0	10.8	6.8	23.2	20.1	3.8	4.5	9.4	3.3	2.3	2.7	13.8
1958	100.0	10.3	6.8	23.5	19.5	4.1	4.3	9.5	3.6	2.4	2.5	13.4
1959	100.0	11.1	6.3	23.3	19.3	4.3	4.3	9.4	3.6	2.2	2.5	13.7
1960	100.0	12.2	6.5	23.9	18.5	5.1	4.1	8.7	3.4	2.3	2.3	12.9
1961	100.0	12.4	6.5	23.7	18.0	5.3	4.1	8.6	3.3	2.6	2.4	13.1
1962	100.0	13.3	6.4	24.9	17.8	5.2	3.6	8.1	3.1	2.5	2.2	12.9
1963	100.0	13.4	6.8	25.0	17.4	5.1	4.0	8.0	3.1	2.7	2.1	12.3
1964	100.0	14.1	7.0	25.1	16.7	4.9	4.1	7.9	3.0	2.7	2.0	12.5
1965	100.0	14.0	7.4	25.7	16.5	4.9	4.0	7.7	2.9	2.8	1.9	12.1
1966	100.0	14.6	6.9	26.8	15.7	5.2	3.8	7.6	2.8	2.8	1.9	11.8
1967	100.0	15.4	7.0	27.9	15.2	5.1	3.7	7.2	2.7	2.5	1.8	11.6
1968	100.0	17.1	6.9	28.7	14.2	5.2	3.5	6.8	2.5	2.4	1.7	10.9
1969	100.0	18.0	7.6	29.7	13.5	4.9	3.3	6.4	2.3	2.4	1.5	10.5
1970	100.0	19.1	7.8	29.6	13.1	4.8	3.2	5.7	2.3	2.1	1.4	10.9
1971	100.0	19.7	6.6	30.0	12.9	4.9	3.2	5.7	2.2	2.1	1.4	11.2
1972	100.0	21.7	7.4	29.4	12.1	4.7	3.0	5.6	2.1	2.2	1.3	10.6
1973	100.0	22.9	8.0	29.1	11.8	4.6	2.9	5.3	1.9	2.1	1.2	10.1
1974	100.0	23.0	8.1	30.5	11.1	4.4	2.8	5.1	1.8	1.9	1.7	9.8
1975	100.0	23.5	8.3	30.9	10.3	4.1	2.6	4.9	1.8	1.8	2.2	9.6
1976	100.0	24.0	8.1	30.6	9.7	3.9	2.5	4.9	2.4	1.7	2.3	9.9
1977	100.0	25.2	9.1	30.6	9.0	3.5	2.3	4.5	2.2	1.8	2.1	9.7
1978	100.0	25.7	9.5	31.1	8.4	3.2	2.2	4.3	2.1	1.6	2.2	9.7

Year	Total	Individual Income	Corporate Income	General Sales, Use or Gross Receipts	Motor Fuels	Tobacco	Alcohol Sales and Licenses	Motor Vehicle and Operators' Licenses	Property	Death and Gift	Severance	Other
1979	100.0	26.1	9.7	31.6	8.0	2.9	2.1	4.1	2.0	1.6	2.3	9.6
1980	100.0	27.1	9.7	31.5	7.1	2.7	1.9	3.9	2.1	1.5	3.0	9.5
1981	100.0	27.3	9.4	31.0	6.5	2.6	1.9	3.8	2.0	1.5	4.3	9.7
1982	100.0	28.1	8.6	31.0	6.4	2.4	1.8	3.7	1.9	1.4	4.8	9.8
1983	100.0	29.0	7.7	31.3	6.3	2.3	1.7	3.7	1.9	1.5	4.3	10.3
1984	100.0	30.0	7.9	31.8	6.3	2.0	1.6	3.5	2.0	1.1	3.7	10.2
1985	100.0	29.6	8.2	32.3	6.2	2.1	1.5	3.6	1.8	1.1	3.3	10.3
1986	100.0	9.6	8.1	32.8	6.2	2.0	1.4	3.7	1.9	1.1	2.7	10.6
1987	100.0	30.8	8.4	32.4	6.4	1.9	1.4	3.7	1.9	1.2	1.6	10.4
1988	100.0	30.3	8.2	32.9	6.5	1.8	1.3	3.7	1.9	1.2	1.6	10.5
1989	100.0	31.2	8.4	32.8	6.3	1.8	1.2	3.6	1.9	1.2	1.5	10.1
1990	100.0	32.0	2.7	33.2	6.4	1.8	1.1	3.6	1.9	1.3	1.6	9.8
1991	100.0	32.0	6.6	33.2	6.6	1.9	1.2	3.5	2.0	1.4	1.7	9.9
1992	100.0	31.8	6.6	32.8	6.8	1.9	1.1	3.6	2.0	1.4	1.4	10.6

[a]Unallocable, included in "Other."
Source: Tax Foundation, Inc. *Facts and Figures on Government Finance*. Washington, 1994. p. 187-188.

APPENDIX I. FEDERAL TAX COLLECTIONS BY TYPE OF TAX

Table I1. Federal Tax Collections by Type of Tax, Selected Fiscal Years 1960-1993

Type of Tax	1960	1970	1980	1990	1991	1992e	1993e
	Amount (U.S. $ millions)						
Total	$90,514	$187,689	$500,933	$999,586	$1,027,023	$1,049,647	$1,139,697
Individual Income Tax	40,715	90,412	244,069	466,884	467,827	478,827	515,195
Corporate Income Tax	21,494	32,829	64,600	93,507	98,086	89,031	103,816
Payroll Taxes[a]	11,248	39,133	138,748	353,891	370,526	383,663	416,003
Unemployment Taxes[b]	2,667	3,470	15,336	21,635	20,922	22,547	25,600
Excise Taxes	11,676	15,705	24,329	35,345	42,402	46,098	48,091
Estate and Gift Taxes	1,606	3,644	6,389	11,500	11,138	12,063	12,872
Customs Duties	1,105	2,430	7,174	16,707	15,949	17,260	17,961
Miscellaneous Taxes	3	66	288	117	173	158	159
	Percentage Distribution						
All Taxes	100.0%	100.0%	100.0%	100.0%	100.0%	100.0%	100.0%
Individual Income Tax	45.0	48.2	48.7	46.7	45.6	45.6	45.2

Type of Tax	1960	1970	1980	1990	1991	1992e	1993e
Corporate Income Tax	23.7	17.5	12.9	9.4	9.6	8.5	9.1
Payroll Taxes	12.4	20.9	27.7	35.4	36.1	36.6	36.5
Unemployment Taxes	2.9	1.8	3.1	2.2	2.0	2.1	2.2
Excise Taxes	12.9	8.4	4.9	3.5	4.1	4.4	4.2
Estate and Gift Taxes	1.8	1.9	1.3	1.2	1.1	1.1	1.1
Customs Duties	1.2	1.3	1.4	1.7	1.6	1.6	1.6
Miscellaneous Taxes	—	—	.1	—	—	—	—

[a]Old–age, survivors, disability, and hospital insurance; and railroad retirement.
[b]Includes State taxes deposited in Treasury.
Source: Tax Foundation, Inc. *Facts and Figures on Government Finance*. Washington, 1993. p. 113.

Appendix J. Sales Tax Rates By State

Table J1. Sales Tax Rates by State, as of January 1994

State	General Sales and Use Tax (percent)
Alabama	4
Alaska	0
Arizona	5
Arkansas	4.5
California	6
Colorado	3
Connecticut	6
Delaware	0
District of Columbia	6
Florida	6
Georgia	5/6
Hawaii	4
Idaho	5
Illinois	6.25
Indiana	5
Iowa	5
Kansas	4.9
Kentucky	6
Louisiana	4
Maine	6
Maryland	5
Massachusetts	5
Michigan	4
Minnesota	6.5
Mississippi	7
Missouri	4.225
Montana	0
Nebraska	5
Nevada	6.5/7
New Hampshire	0
New Jersey	6
New Mexico	5
New York	4

State	General Sales and Use Tax (percent)
North Carolina	4
North Dakota	5
Ohio	5
Oklahoma	4.5
Oregon	0
Pennsylvania	6
Rhode Island	7
South Carolina	5
South Dakota	4
Tennessee	6
Texas	6.25
Utah	6
Vermont	5
Virginia	3.5
Washington	6.5
West Virginia	6
Wisconsin	5
Wyoming	4

Source: Adapted by CRS from Tax Foundation Inc. *Facts and Figures on Government Finance*. Washington, 1994. p. 201.

APPENDIX K. SURVEYS OF PUBLIC OPINION

ACIR Survey

The Advisory Commission on Intergovernmental Relations contracted with Gallup to survey the public on the following question: "If the Federal Government had to raise taxes substantially, which would be a better way to do it?"[70] The three possible responses were: (1) increasing individual income taxes; (2) a new national sales tax on all purchases other than food; and (3) don't know.[71] This survey may be particularly relevant since the choice for a Federal tax increase may be between a value–added tax and higher Federal income taxes.

---

[70] Advisory Commission on Intergovernmental Relations. *Changing Attitudes on Governments and Taxes*. Washington, 1983. p. 4.
[71] Ibid.

Value-Added Tax: Concepts, Policy Issues, and OECD Experiences 55

From April 29 through May 2, 1983, personal interviews were conducted in the homes of a sample of 1,517 men and women 18 years and over. The results were weighted using demographic factors so that they could be projected to the total adult civilian population. The survey results are accurate within a three percent margin of error at a 95 percent level of confidence.[72]

Data in table K1 show both aggregate results and detailed results based on demographic factors. For the total public, 24 percent favored increasing individual income taxes, 52 percent favored a new national sales tax on all purchases other than food, and 25 percent did not know. Regardless of the demographic characteristics considered, a statistically significant percent of respondents preferred a new national sales tax over an increase in individual income taxes with a substantial proportion not knowing. The demographic characteristics considered were sex, head of household, age, level of education, household income, home ownership status, race, employment status, occupation, marital status, household size, children in household, region, and nonmetro/metro status.[73]

The ACIR survey is the only survey in which the public was asked to only select between increasing individual income taxes and establishing a new national sales tax (on all purchases other than food). The ACIR survey also has a detailed breakdown of public opinion by characteristics of households. But the ACIR survey occurred in 1983, and public opinion may change over time.

TableK1. If the Federal Government Had to Raise Taxes Substantially, Which Would Be a Better Way to Do It? (in percent)

	Increasing Individual Income Taxes	A New National Sales Tax on All Purchases Other than Food	Don't Know
Total Public	24	52	25
Male	25	53	22
Female	23	51	27
Head of Household	24	51	25
Male Head	27	52	22
Female Head	22	51	27
Under 35 Years of	26	52	22

---

[72] Ibid.
[73] Ibid., p. 9.

	Increasing Individual Income Taxes	A New National Sales Tax on All Purchases Other than Food	Don't Know
Age			
18-24	24	56	20
25-34	27	49	24
35-44	22	56	23
45-65	24	52	24
Over 65	21	44	35
High School Incomplete	19	47	35
High School Graduate	22	55	23
College Incomplete	26	59	15
College Graduate	37	46	17
Household Income			
Under $15K	22	47	32
$15-24.9K	23	54	23
$25K+	28	58	15
$25-29.9K	29	55	16
$30-39.9K	28	60	12
$40K+	26	58	17
Own	23	54	22
Rent	25	45	30
White	25	52	23
Nonwhite	16	49	36
Employed	27	53	20
Employed Female	30	49	21
Not Employed	20	50	30
Not Employed Female	18	52	30
Prof. Manager, Owner	29	53	18
White Collar, Sales, Clerical	28	52	20
Blue Collar	20	55	25
Retired	27	44	30
Married	25	54	22
Not Married	23	48	29
Household			
1-2 People	25	50	26

	Increasing Individual Income Taxes	A New National Sales Tax on All Purchases Other than Food	Don't Know
3-4 People	25	53	22
5+ People	21	54	26
Children in Household			
Children under 18	22	54	24
No Children	25	50	25
Northeast	31	40	29
North-Central	21	58	21
South	21	55	24
West	24	52	25
Nonmetro	21	57	22
Metro—50,000 and Over			
Fringe	27	50	23
Central City	25	46	30

Source: Advisory Commission on Intergovernmental Relations. *Changing Public Attitudes on Governments and Taxes.* Washington, 1983. p. 9.

Media General/Associated Press Poll

Between November 10 and November 20, 1988, Media General Research conducted a public opinion poll for Media General/Associated Press. A representative sample of 1,084 adults were called by telephone from listed and unlisted telephones. Men accounted for 48 percent of the sample and women for 52 percent.[74]

The sample was asked the following question:

- Here are some possible ways for the Government to raise money to reduce the Federal budget deficit. For each, please tell me whether you support or oppose it.

The public's responses concerning a national sales tax and higher personal income taxes were[75]

Table K2. Tax Increases to Reduce the Deficit

---

[74] Media General/Associated Press Poll. Richmond, Media General, November 20, 1988. p. 1.
[75] Ibid., p. 2.

Answer	Support	Oppose	Don't Know Or No
A National Sales Tax	29%	64%	7%
Higher Personal Income Taxes	15%	80%	4%

Source: Media General/Associated Press Poll. Richmond, Media General, November 20, 1988. p. 2.

Thus, this poll found that the public support for a NST was approximately double that of an increase in personal income taxes, although both taxes were opposed by substantial majorities.

The Harris Poll

Between December 2 and 6, 1988, a Harris Poll was conducted by telephone using a nationwide sample of 1,248 adults. The results of a poll this size have a 95 percent probability of being within three percent of the opinions of the entire adult population.[76]

The nationwide sample was asked the following question:

Now let me ask you about specific tax increases that some people feel are necessary to balance the Federal budget and end deficit spending. In each case, the Congress would pass a tax increase that would make sure none of the money raised from added taxes would be used for additional spending. Instead, all of the new tax money would have to be used to reduce the Federal deficit. This tax would be in effect for only three years. If (read specific tax) combined with spending reductions would eliminate the Federal deficit in three years, would you favor or oppose that tax?[77]

The sample's answers to this question for a national sales tax or a 10 percent surcharge on Federal income taxes are shown in table K3. Individuals favored a NST over an income tax surcharge by approximately a two to one margin. This approximately two to one margin also existed for those individuals who voted for Bush and those who voted for Dukakis.[78]

---

[76] The Harris Poll. Creators Syndicator, Inc., Los Angeles, January 8, 1989. p. 1.
[77] Ibid.
[78] Ibid., p. 2.

Table K3. Tax Increases to Balance the Federal Budget

	Favor	Oppose	Not Sure
A National Sales Tax			
Total	47%	50%	3%
Voted for Bush in 1988	52%	45%	3%
Voted for Dukakis in 1988	44%	54%	2%
A 10 percent surcharge on Federal Income Taxes			
Total	24%	71%	5%
Voted for Bush in 1988	27%	68%	5%
Voted for Dukakis in 1988	23%	73%	4%

Source: The Harris Poll. Creators Syndicator, Inc. Los Angeles, January 8, 1989. p. 2.

SELECTED BIBLIOGRAPHY

Aaron, Henry J. The political economy of a value–added tax in the United States. Tax notes, v. 38, no. 10, March 7, 1988: 1,111–1,115.

-----, ed. The value–added tax: lessons from Europe. Washington, The Brookings Institution, 1981. 107 p.

----- The value–added tax: sorting through the practical and political problems. The Brookings review, v. 6, summer 1988: 10–16.

Advisory Commission on Intergovernmental Relations. Changing public attitudes on government and taxes. Washington, 1983. 59 p.

----- Significant Features of Fiscal Federalism: Budget Processes and Tax Systems. Washington, June 1994. 170 p.

Brashares, Edith, Janet Furman Speyrer, and George N. Carlson. Distributional aspects of a Federal value–added tax. National tax journal, v. 41, no. 2, June 1988: 155–173.

Caspersen, Erik and Gilbert Metcalf. Is a value–added tax progressive? Annual versus lifetime incidence measures. National tax journal, v. 47, no. 1, December 1994: 731-746.

Center for Cooperation with European Economics in Transition. The role of tax reform in center and Eastern European economies. Paris, Organization for Economic Cooperation and Development, 1991. 458 p.

Clinton signs FY1994 appropriations budget for IRS, Treasury, Postal Service. Daily tax report, November 1, 1993. p. G4–G5.

Cnossen, Sijbren. Key questions in considering a value–added tax for Central and Eastern European countries. IMF staff papers, v. 39, no. 2, June 1992: 211–255.

----- The value–added tax: questions and answers. Tax notes, v. 42, no. 2, January 9, 1989: 209–213.

Commission of the European Communities. A single market for goods. Luxembourg, 1993. 9 p.

Due, John F. Some unresolved issues in design and implementation of value–added taxes. National tax journal, v. 43, no. 4, December, 1990: 383–394.

----- and John L. Mikesell. Sales taxation: State and local structure and administration. Baltimore, Johns Hopkins University Press, 1983. 350 p.

Focus on the value–added tax. Washington, Coopers & Lybrand, 1986. 34 p.

Gravelle, Jane G. Assessing a value–added tax: efficiency and equity. Tax notes, v. 38, no. 10, March 7, 1988: 1,117–1,123.

----- Income, consumption, and wage taxation in a life–cycle model: separating efficiency from redistribution. American economic review, vol. 81, no. 4, September 1991: 985–995.

Gillis, Malcolm, Carl S. Shoup, and Gerardo P. Sicat, eds. Value–added taxation in developing countries. Washington, World Bank, 1990. 237 p.

Harris Poll. Los Angeles, Creators Syndicator, Inc., January 8, 1989. 2 p.

Hart, Craig A. The European Community's value-added tax system: analysis of the new transitional regime and prospectives for further harmonization. International tax and business lawyer, v. 12, no. 1, 1994: 1-62.

Internal Revenue Service. Income tax compliance research: net tax gap and remittance gap estimates. Washington, April 1990. 18 p.

Kotlikoff, Laurence J. Intergenerational transfers and savings. Journal of economic perspectives, v. 2, no. 2, spring 1988: 41–58.

Marvin, Rob and Vandana Mathur. Status quo budget for IRS proposes 9.8% increase over 11995. Daily Tax Report, no. 25, February 7, 1995. p. G6–G7.

McLure, Charles, Jr. The value–added tax: key to deficit reduction? Washington, American Enterprise Institute for Public Policy Research, 1987. 184 p.

Media General/Associated Press Poll. Richmond, Media General, November 20, 1988. 5 p.

Modigliani, Franco. The role of intergenerational transfers and life cycle saving in the accumulation of wealth. Journal of economic perspectives, v. 2, no. 2, spring 1988: 15–40.

Musgrave, Richard A., and Peggy B. Musgrave. Public finance in theory and practice. 4th ed. New York, McGraw–Hill, 1984. 824 p.

Rivlin, Alice M. Reviving the American dream. Washington, The Brookings Institution, 1992. 196 p.

Rushton, Michael. A value-added tax for the United States: lessons from the Canadian experience. National Tax Association–Proceedings of the eighty-sixth annual conference, 1993. p. 96-100.

Rose, Harold. The question of saving. London, British–North American Committee, 1991. 53 p.

Tait, Alan A. Value–added tax: international practice and problems. Washington, International Monetary Fund, 1988. 450 p.

Tax Foundation Inc. Facts and figures on government finance. Washington, 1993. 352 p.

-----. Facts and figures on government finance. Washington, 1994. 272 p.

Tax Executive Institute. Value–added taxes: a comparative analysis. Washington, 1992. 141 p.

Taxing consumption. Paris, Organization for Economic Cooperation and Development, 1988. 335 p.

Taxation in OECD countries. Paris, Organization for Economic Cooperation and Development, 1993. 112 p.

Turner, William J. Designing an efficient value–added tax. Tax law review, v. 39, no. 2, summer 1984: 435–472.

----- VAT: minimizing administrative and compliance costs. Tax notes, v. 38, no. 11, March 14, 1988: 1,257–1,268.

U.S. Congress. Joint Committee on Taxation. Description of tax bills: S. 353 (Educational savings bond); S. 442 (Value–added tax); S. 659, S. 838, S. 849 (Estate freezer); and S. 800 (Moratorium on certain State tax laws). Washington, U.S. Govt. Print. Off., 1989. p. 1–2, 6–31.

U.S. Congressional Budget Office. Assessing the decline in the national saving rate. Washington, April 1993. 44 p.

----- Effects of adopting a value–added tax. Washington, February 1992. 79 p.

U.S. Department of the Treasury. Office of the Secretary. Tax reform for fairness, simplicity, and economic growth. v. 3, Value–added tax. [Washington] November 1984. 128 p.

U.S. General Accounting Office. Budget policy: prompt action necessary to avert long–term damage to the economy. Washington, June 1992. 116 p.

----- Value–added tax: administrative costs vary with complexity and number of businesses. Washington, May 1993. 159 p.

----- State tax officials have concerns about a Federal consumption tax. Washington, March 1990. 77 p.

U.S. Library of Congress. Congressional Research Service. A value–added tax contrasted with a national sales tax, by James M. Bickley. [Washington] 1992. (Updated regularly) CRS Issue Brief No. IB92069

----- Economic effects of a value–added tax on capital formation, by Jane G. Gravelle. [Washington] 1988. 14 p. CRS Report No. 88–697 S

----- Economic effects of a VAT on small business, by James M. Bickley. [Washington] 1988. 23 p. CRS Report No. 88–288 E

----- Value–added tax in Canada: background, evaluation, and implications for the United States, by James M. Bickley. [Washington] April 14, 1993. 12 p. CRS Report No. 93–405 E

----- Value–added tax: revenue estimates for FY95, by James M. Bickley. [Washington] 1993. 13 p. CRS Report No. 93–687 E

----- Value–added tax: should it be calculated by the credit–invoice or subtraction method? by James M. Bickley. [Washington] June 15, 1992. 12 p. CRS Report No. 92–504 E

----- Value–added tax as a new revenue source, by James M. Bickley. [Washington] 1991. (Updated regularly) CRS Issue Brief No. IB91078

Chapter 2

A VALUE-ADDED TAX CONTRASTED WITH A NATIONAL SALES TAX

SUMMARY

Proposals to replace all or part of the income tax and proposals for national health care have sparked congressional interest in the possibility of a broad-based consumption tax as a new source of revenue. Both a value-added tax (VAT) and a national sales tax (NST) have been considered by some Members of Congress.

A firm's value added for a product is the increase in the value of that product caused by the application of the firm's factors of production. A VAT on a product would be levied at all stages of production of that product. A firm's net VAT liability is usually calculated by using the credit method. According to this method, a firm determines its gross tax liability by multiplying its sales by the VAT rate. Then the firm computes its net VAT liability by subtracting VAT paid on purchases from other firms from the firm's gross VAT liability.

The three types of VAT differ in their tax treatment of purchases of capital (plant and equipment). A consumption VAT treats a firm's purchases of plant and equipment the same way as any other purchase by a firm. All developed nations with VAT have the consumption type. The other two types of VATs are the income VAT and the gross product VAT. Under the income VAT, the VAT paid on the purchases of capital inputs is amortized (credited against the firm's VAT liability) over the expected lives of the capital inputs. Under the gross product VAT, no deduction for the VAT on purchases of capital inputs is allowed against the firm's VAT liability. A

NST would be a federal consumption tax collected only at the retail level by vendors. Both a VAT and a NST are assumed to be ultimately paid by consumers. For FY2000, a broad-based VAT or NST would have raised net revenue of approximately $37.8 billion for each 1% levied.

The operating differences between a consumption VAT and a NST have important policy implications. The administrative cost of a VAT would exceed that of a NST because a VAT would require more information to be reported and audited. An opportunity exists for a NST to be collected jointly with state sales taxes, but a federal VAT offers no readily available joint collection possibilities. A consumption VAT with the credit method more easily excludes inputs from double taxation than does a NST. A consumption VAT would be easier to enforce than a NST. It is in the self-interest of a firm to have accurate purchase invoices so that it can obtain full credit for prior VAT paid. Tax authorities can double check the accuracy of the VAT remitted by any firm because data are collected from producers at all levels of production. A VAT could have a broader tax base than a NST because a VAT is easier to enforce. A VAT could have a higher tax rate than a NST because a VAT is more difficult to evade. A VAT would require more time to implement than a NST because a VAT is more complicated, covers more firms, and is a new tax method. A VAT may be less visible to consumers than a NST. A VAT is levied at all stages of production, and policymakers have the option of not requiring the amount of VAT to be shown on retail sales receipts.

MOST RECENT DEVELOPMENTS

On October 8, 2002, at a National Bureau of Economic Research conference, Randall Kroszner from the Council of Economic Advisers stated that the Bush Administration was examining the concept of shifting our federal income tax system to a consumption based tax system.

BACKGROUND AND ANALYSIS

Proposals to replace all or part of the income tax and proposals for national health care have sparked congressional interest in possible sources of additional revenue. A value-added tax (VAT) or a national sales tax (NST) have been frequently discussed as possible new tax sources. Both the VAT and the NST are taxes on the consumption of goods and services and are conceptually similar. Yet, these taxes also have significant differences. This issue brief discusses some of the potential policy implications associated with these differences.

Concept of a Value-Added Tax

The value added of a firm is the difference between a firm's sales and a firm's purchases from all other firms. In other words, a firm's value added is simply the amount of value that a firm contributes to a good or service by applying its factors of production (land, labor, capital, and entrepreneurial ability). A value-added tax would be a tax, levied at each stage of production, on a firm's net value added. The credit method is usually used to collect the VAT. Under the credit method, a firm would calculate the VAT on its sales. Next, a firm would compute its VAT liability by subtracting the VAT paid on its inputs from the VAT on its sales, and would then remit the difference to the federal government to cover its tax liability.

There are three types of VATs which differ in their tax treatment of purchases of capital inputs (plant and equipment). The consumption-type VAT treats capital purchases the same way as the purchase of any other input, i.e., it is equivalent to expensing. The other two types of VATs are the income VAT and the gross product VAT. Under the income VAT, the VAT paid on the purchases of capital inputs is amortized (credit against the firm's VAT liability) over the expected lives of the capital inputs. Under the gross product VAT, no deduction for the VAT on purchases of capital inputs is allowed against the firm's VAT liability. The consumption VAT is the only type of VAT that is used in developed nations and has been proposed for the United States; consequently, the consumption VAT is contrasted with the NST in this issue brief.

A National Sales Tax

A national sales tax (NST) would be a federal consumption tax collected only at the retail level by vendors. The NST would equal a set percentage of the retail price of taxable goods and services. Retail vendors would collect the NST and remit tax revenue to the federal government.

The retail price of a good or service equals the sum of value added at all stages of production. Consequently, a value-added tax and a national sales tax with the same tax rate and tax base would yield the same amount of revenue. The operating assumption of policymakers and economists is that both taxes are fully shifted forward onto consumers; that is, the price to the consumer increases by the (full) amount of the tax. For FY2000, a broad-based VAT would have raised net revenue of approximately $37.8 billion for each 1% levied.

Policy Implications

The operating differences between a VAT and a NST have many important policy implications, including the following eight factors: administrative cost, joint tax collections, avoiding double taxation of intermediate goods and services, enforcement, broadness of tax base, maximum tax rate, time required to implement, and visibility.

Administrative Costs

Under a VAT, all firms would have to report tax information and collect taxes. Under a NST, firms without retail sales would not report or collect taxes. But the substantial majority of all firms would collect the NST since they have some retail sales. Under a VAT with a credit method of collection, each firm must keep invoices on all sales and purchases from other firms, and these invoices would be subject to audit by tax authorities. Hence, the value-added tax would require more information to be reported and audited than a national sales tax, and, consequently, a VAT could be expected to be more expensive to administer than a NST.

Joint Tax Collection

Since 45 states and the District of Columbia have general sales taxes, an opportunity exists for a NST to be collected jointly with state sales taxes. A federal VAT could not be jointly collected with state sales taxes. States could convert their sales taxes to a VAT with the federal tax base, but this is unlikely since it would require that the states establish an entirely new tax system. Consequently, no administrative costs saving would be expected from a VAT; therefore, the collection costs of a VAT can be expected to be higher than a NST.

Avoiding Double Taxation of Intermediate Goods and Services

Double taxation occurs if an input is taxed at the time of purchase and then a tax is levied on the same input again when it becomes part of the output of the firm. A consumption VAT, with the credit method of tax computation, easily excludes inputs from taxation. The exclusion of inputs from a NST would be more difficult. Usually, firms buying inputs would have to provide sellers with exemption certificates before making their purchases. At the state level, procedures to exempt input purchases from state retail sales taxes have worked imperfectly. It is therefore reasonable to expect that excluding inputs from taxation would be more difficult with a NST than with a VAT.

Enforcement

With a VAT, a firm would have a financial interest in ensuring that amounts of VAT paid on input purchases are accurately reported on its purchase invoices since the firm could receive credits against its VAT liability. In addition, the VAT would provide the tax authorities with an opportunity to cross-check the amount of VAT collected because data are gathered from producers at different stages of production. Some enforcement problems do exist with a VAT. For example, firms at different stages of production could collude to falsify invoices. But the NST lacks both the self-enforcing procedure and the cross-checking opportunity of the VAT. Hence, better compliance is expected from a VAT than with a NST.

Broadness of Tax Base

Because of the potential for better enforcement of a VAT, it may be possible to levy a VAT on more goods and services than a NST. This view is supported by the fact that VATs of European nations, on the average, are levied on more goods and services than most state sales taxes in the United States.

Maximum Tax Rate

Both the self-enforcing procedure and the cross-checking opportunity of a VAT would increase the probability of a tax evader being apprehended. Thus, for a given tax rate, a VAT is expected to have better voluntary compliance than a NST. In general, as a tax rate rises, the financial gains from tax evasion increase relative to the punishment if apprehended. Consequently, it is expected that as a consumption tax rate is increased, the level of tax evasion would rise. Since voluntary compliance with a VAT is expected to be better than with a NST, the tax rate for a VAT may be raised to a higher level than for a NST before a problem with tax evasion occurs.

Time Required to Implement

The VAT would take more time to implement than a NST. The VAT is more complicated and would cover more firms than a NST. Also, business executives are not familiar with this form of taxation, so the U.S. government would have to conduct an educational campaign.

Visibility

The value-added tax may be less visible to consumers than a national sales tax. Policymakers and economists assume that 100% of both the VAT and the NST are passed onto consumers. But the perceptions of many consumers may be different about a VAT. Many consumers may believe that a VAT tax would at least partially fall on firms because the VAT is collected at each stage of production. Since the NST is levied only at the retail level, consumers may more readily believe that they would pay the entire tax. Furthermore, policymakers have the option as to whether or not the amount of a VAT should be stated on retail sales receipts. The amount of a NST would be explicitly stated on sales receipts.

The lower visibility of the VAT relative to the NST may be either desirable or undesirable depending on one's political ideology. It can be argued that taxes should be visible so that the costs of taxation may be compared with the benefits of government spending. Conversely, it can be argued that people generally do not like the idea of paying taxes; consequently, to finance public sector responsibilities, it is better to have taxes seem as painless as possible.

LEGISLATION

H.R. 86 (English)

Simplified USA Tax Act of 2001. Replaces the individual income tax, the corporate income tax, and the estate and gift taxes with a border-adjustable business tax (subtraction-method VAT) and a progressive consumed-income tax. Individuals may utilize the equivalent of universal Roth IRAs to encourage savings. Introduced January 3, 2001; referred to House Committee on Ways and Means.

H.R. 1040 (Armey)

Freedom and Fairness Restoration Act of 2001. (H.R. 1040 and S. 1040 are identical bills.) Repeals the corporate income tax, the individual income tax, and the estate and gift tax; and replaces these taxes with a flat rate consumption tax of 17%. Introduced March 15, 2001; referred to the Committee on Ways and Means and the Committee on Rules.

H.R. 2525 (Linder)

Fair Tax Act of 2001. Repeals the individual income tax, the corporate income tax, all payroll taxes, the self-employment tax, and the estate and gift taxes and levies a 23% national retail sales tax as a replacement. Every family would receive a rebate of the sales tax on spending up to the federal poverty level (plus an extra amount to prevent any marriage penalty). Introduced July 17, 2001; referred to the House Committee on Ways and Means.

H.R. 2717 (Tauzin)

Individual Tax Freedom Act of 2001. Effective July 1, 2003, levies a 15% national retail sales tax as a replacement for the individual and corporate income taxes, the estate and gift taxes, and certain excise taxes. This national retail sales tax would be administered primarily be the states. Introduced August 2, 2001; referred to the House Committee on Ways and Means and the House Rules Committee.

H.R. 4716 (DeMint)

Date Certain Tax Code Replacement Act. Establishes within the legislative branch a National Commission on Tax Reform and Simplification that shall review and and submit to Congress a report on (1) the present structure and provisions of the Internal Revenue Code; (2) whether tax systems imposed under the laws of other countries could provide more efficient, simple, and fair methods of funding the revenue requirements of the government; (3) whether the income tax should be replaced with a tax imposed in a different manner or on a different base; and (4) whether the Internal Revenue Code can be simplified, absent wholesale restructuring or replacement. Authorizes appropriations for the Commission. Any new federal tax system would require approval by Congress no later than July 4, 2005. If a new federal tax system is not approved by July 4, 2005, then Congress would be required to vote to reauthorize the Internal Revenue Code of 1986. Introduced May 14, 2002; referred to the House Committee on Ways and Means.

S. 1040 (Shelby)

Freedom and Fairness Restoration Act of 2001. (H.R. 1040 and S. 1040 are identical bills.) Repeals the corporate income tax, the individual income tax, and the estate and gift tax; and replaces these taxes with a flat rate consumption tax of 17%. Introduced June 14, 2001; referred to the Committee on Finance.

Chapter 3

VALUE-ADDED TAX AS A NEW REVENUE SOURCE

SUMMARY

Some Members of Congress have expressed interest in the feasibility of using a value-added tax (VAT) to either replace all or part of the income tax or finance health care reform. A VAT is imposed at all levels of production on the differences between firms' sales and their purchases from all other firms. Policymakers may be interested in the following aspects of a VAT: revenue yield, international comparison of composition of taxes, vertical equity, neutrality, inflation, balance-of-trade, national saving, administrative cost, intergovernmental relations, size of government, and public opinion.

For FY2000 a broad-based VAT would have raised net revenue of approximately $37.8 billion for each 1% levied. Most other developed nations rely more for revenue on broad-based consumption taxes than does the United States. A VAT is shifted onto consumers and, consequently, is regressive because lower-income households spend a greater proportion of their incomes on consumption than higher-income households. This regression could be reduced or even eliminated by any of three methods: a refundable credit against income tax liability for VAT paid, allocation of some of VAT revenue for increased welfare spending, or selective exclusion of some goods from taxation.

From an economic perspective, a major revenue source is better the greater its neutrality, that is, the less the tax alters economic decisions. A VAT is a relatively, but not completely, neutral tax. A VAT cannot be levied on all goods; consequently, a VAT would raise the prices of taxed goods relative to untaxed goods. This change in relative prices would distort households' choices among goods. A VAT cannot be levied on leisure; consequently, a VAT would affect households' decisions concerning work versus leisure.

The imposition of a VAT would cause a one-time increase in this country's price level. But a VAT would not affect this country's future rate of inflation if the Federal Reserve offset the contractionary effects of a VAT with a more expansionary monetary policy. If the United States continued its policy of flexible exchange rates, then the imposition of a VAT would not significantly affect the U.S. balance-of-trade. There is no conclusive evidence that a VAT would increase the rate of national saving more than another type of major tax increase.

The high revenue yield from a VAT would cause administrative costs to be low measured as a percentage of revenue yield. A federal VAT would encroach on the primary source of state revenue, the sales tax. But precedents exist for the federal government to levy a tax that some states have already imposed. A federal-state VAT could be collected jointly, but a state would lose some of its fiscal discretion. The hypothesis that a federal VAT would increase the size of the U.S. government has not been proven empirically.

MOST RECENT DEVELOPMENTS

On October 8, 2002, at a National Bureau of Economic Research conference, Randall Kroszner from the Council of Economic Advisers stated that the Bush Administration was examining the concept of shifting our federal income tax system to a consumption based tax system.

BACKGROUND AND ANALYSIS

Proposals to replace all or part of the income tax system with a consumption tax and proposals for national health care have caused Members of Congress to consider different tax options that would yield large amounts of revenue. The value-added tax (VAT), a broad-based consumption tax, is the subject of congressional interest.

The value-added of a firm is the difference between that firm's sales and its purchases from all other firms. A VAT is levied on firms' value added at all stages of production. For FY2000, a VAT imposed on most goods and services could have raised a net revenue of approximately $37.8 billion for each 1% rate levied.

Aspects of a VAT that often raise interest or concern include: revenue yield, international comparison of composition of taxes, administrative cost, vertical equity, neutrality, inflation, balance-of-trade, national saving, administrative cost, intergovernmental relations, and size of government. This issue brief considers the experiences of the 28 nations (out of 29 nations) with VATs in the Organization for Economic Cooperation and Development (OECD) relevant to the feasibility and operation of a possible U.S. VAT. The OECD consists of 21 European nations, Turkey, the United States, Canada, Australia, New Zealand, Japan, Mexico, and South Korea.

Revenue Yield

The primary reason for considering a VAT for financing health care reform or replacing all or part of our income tax system is its enormous revenue potential. Economists and public officials use the operating assumption that a VAT would be fully shifted to final consumers in the form of higher prices of goods. A VAT (or any other major tax increase) would have a contractionary effect on the economy unless offset by other economic policies. Consequently, the revenue estimates in this issue brief are made under the assumption that the Federal Reserve would use an expansionary monetary policy to neutralize the contractionary effects of a VAT. These revenue estimates also do not take into account the possible shifts in consumption patterns that might be expected if some items are taxed and others are excluded from taxation.

The potential revenue per 1.0% rate from a VAT would vary with the comprehensiveness of the tax base. A broad-based VAT would have limited exclusions, while a narrow-based VAT would have numerous exclusions. Obviously, the broader the tax base, the lower the tax rate necessary to raise a given amount of revenue. Furthermore, the broader the VAT base, the more efficient the tax system. For fiscal year 2000, each 1.0% rate for a VAT could have raised net revenue of approximately $37.8 billion with a broad base and net revenue of approximately $20.0 billion with a narrow base.

International Comparison of Composition of Taxes

One argument frequently made for a U.S. VAT is the relative reliance on consumption taxes in other developed countries. Most other developed nations do rely more on consumption taxes. For 1998 the United States (federal, state, and local governments) relied less on taxes on goods and services (14.1% of total tax revenues) than any other nation in the OECD. For 1998, for taxes on general consumption (e.g., VATs and sales taxes), the United States had a lower reliance (7.6% of tax revenues) than any other OECD nation.

Vertical Equity

The vertical equity of a tax concerns the tax treatment of households with different abilities-to-pay. Vertical equity may be affected by the measure of ability-to-pay and the tax period. Some economists argue that personal consumption is the best measure of ability-to-pay because consumption is the actual taking of scarce resources from the economic system. The most common measure of ability-to-pay is still income. Proponents of income as a measure of ability-to-pay argue that saving yields utility by providing households with greater economic security.

Tax incidence usually is measured by using a one-year period. Data on consumption and income are readily available in one-year increments and the concept of a one-year period is easily understood. But some tax economists believe tax incidence is more accurately determined by measuring consumption and income over a household's lifetime.

If consumption is used as a measure of ability-to-pay, a single-rate VAT with a broad base would be approximately proportional regardless of the time period. In other words, the percentage of consumption paid in VAT by households would be approximately constant as the level of household consumption rises.

If disposable income over a one-year period is the measure of ability-to-pay then a VAT would be viewed as extremely regressive; that is, the percentage of disposable income paid in VAT would decrease rapidly as disposable income increases. In most discussions of tax policy, both a one-year period and annual disposable income (or some other annual income measure) are used; consequently, the VAT is viewed as being extremely regressive.

Value-Added Tax as a New Revenue Source   75

If disposable income over a lifetime is the measure of ability-to-pay, a VAT would be mildly regressive. For lower and middle income households, it appears that nearly all savings are eventually consumed. Thus, it may be that for the vast majority of households, lifetime consumption and lifetime income are approximately equal. High income households tend to have net savings over their lifetimes; consequently, they would pay a lower proportion of their disposable incomes in VAT than lower income groups.

Some supporters of progressive taxation oppose the VAT primarily because they believe that it is regressive. Some of these critics are especially concerned about the absolute burden of a VAT on low income households. The degree of regressivity, however, can be reduced by government policy. Three often-mentioned policies are exclusions and multiple rates, income tax credits, and earmarking of some revenues for increased social spending (including indexed transfer payments).

Neutrality

From an economic perspective, the greater a source of revenue's neutrality, the more it is generally preferred; that is, the less it affects economic decisions. Conceptually, a VAT on all consumption expenditures with a single rate that is constant over time would be relatively neutral compared to other major revenue sources.

For households, two out of three major decisions would not be altered by this hypothetical VAT. First, this VAT would not alter choices among goods because all goods would be taxed at the same rate. Thus, relative prices would not change. Second, a VAT would not affect the saving-consumption decision because saving would only be taxed once; that is, when savings are spent on consumption. But the third decision, a household's work-leisure decision, would be affected by a VAT. Leisure would not be taxed, but the returns from work would be taxed when spent on goods. (In contrast, the income tax affects both the saving-consumption decision and the work-leisure decision.)

For a firm, the VAT would not affect decisions concerning method of financing (debt or equity), choice among inputs (unless some suppliers are exempt or zero-rated), type of business organization (corporation, partnership, or sole proprietorship), and goods to produce. Other types of taxes may affect one or more of these types of decisions.

But this conceptually pure form of a VAT is not feasible. A VAT cannot be levied on all consumer goods; consequently, prices of taxed goods will rise relative to untaxed goods. This change in relative prices would affect consumers' decisions about which goods to purchase, and, consequently, firms' decisions about which goods to produce. Furthermore, most nations with VATs have more than one rate. Multiple VAT rates alter relative prices of taxed goods. Finally, VAT rates in most nations have tended to rise over time. Despite these deviations from a pure form of VAT, a broad-based VAT is relatively neutral. This neutrality is greater if the tax rate is relatively low, as could be the case for a VAT to reduce the U.S. deficit.

Inflation

A VAT initially would cause a one-time increase in the price level if the Federal Reserve had an expansionary monetary policy to offset the contractionary effects of the tax. For example, a 4% VAT on 75% of consumer outlays might cause an estimated increase in consumer prices of approximately 3%.

A VAT would have some secondary price effects. Some goods would rise in price because their factors of production, especially labor, are linked to price indexes. Yet, if the Federal Reserve disregarded these secondary price increases in formulating monetary policy, these secondary price increases would tend to be offset by price reductions in other sectors of the economy. In summary, a VAT would probably cause a one-time increase in the price level but not affect the rate of inflation, i.e., increased prices in the future.

Balance-of-Trade

Currently, all nations with VATs zero-rate exports and impose their VATs on imports. This procedure for taxing trade flows is referred to as the destination principle because a commodity is taxed at the location of consumption rather than production. The destination principle creates a level playing field because imported commodities rise in price by the percentage of the VAT, but exported commodities do not increase in price. For a particular nation, the VAT rate on domestically produced and consumed products would be the same. The VAT rate on a particular good would vary among nations.

With flexible exchange rates, the supply and demand for different currencies determine their relative value. If a country has a deficit in its balance-of-trade, this deficit must financed by a net importation of foreign capital. But net capital inflows cannot continue indefinitely. Thus, over time, this country's currency will tend to decline in value relative to the currencies of other nations. Consequently, this country's balance-of-trade deficit will eventually decline as its exports rise and imports fall. Hence, economic theory indicated that a VAT offers no advantage over other major taxes in reducing a deficit in the balance-of-trade.

National Saving

If a VAT is levied to replace part of income tax revenue, what would be the effect on the personal saving rate. A VAT taxes savings when they are spent on consumption, allowing savings to compound at a pre-tax rate. But an income tax is levied on all income at the time it is earned, regardless of whether the income is consumed or saved. The income tax is also levied on the earnings from income saved. Consequently, some proponents of the VAT have argued that choosing a VAT rather than an income tax to raise revenue would increase the return from saving, and, consequently, raise the savings rate.

The rate of return on savings, however, has never been shown to have a significant effect on the savings rate because of two conflicting effects. First, each dollar saved today results in the possibility of a higher amount of consumption in the future. This relative increase in the return from saving causes a household to want to substitute saving for consumption out of current income (substitution effect). But a higher rate of return on savings raises a household's income; consequently, the household has to save less to accumulate some target amount of savings in the future (income effect). Thus, this income effect encourages households to have higher current consumption and lower current saving. In summary, there is no conclusive evidence that a VAT would increase the rate of national saving more than another type of major tax increase.

Administrative Cost

The value-added tax would require the expansion of the Internal Revenue Service. But the high revenue yield from a VAT could cause administrative costs to be low measured as a percentage of revenue yield. The administrative expense per dollar of VAT collected would vary with the degree of complexity of the VAT, the amount of revenue raised, the national attitude towards tax compliance, and the level of the small business exemption. Proposed VATs for deficit reduction usually are estimated to yield approximately $100 billion per fiscal year which would result in the spreading of administrative costs. In 1984, officials at the U.S. Treasury estimated that a completely phased in VAT would require additional staff of 20,694 at a cost of $700 million or approximately $1 billion at 1991 salary levels. For FY1991, the Internal Revenue Service had operating costs of $6.1 billion and average positions realized of 115,628.

Intergovernmental Relations

A federal VAT would encroach on the primary source of state revenue because states would find it more difficult to raise their sales tax rates. But, precedents exist for the federal government to levy a new tax that states have already imposed. For example, the federal government levied death taxes and personal income taxes after many states already had passed them.

The possibility exists for the joint collection of a federal-state VAT. But states would have to replace their sales taxes with VATs with the same tax base as the federal VAT. Consequently, states would lose some of their fiscal discretion.

Size of Government

There is an hypothesis that a relatively hidden tax such as the VAT leads to an expansion in the size of government. A VAT has the capacity to raise enormous revenues at a low tax rate. Households may underestimate their total tax burden because they pay VAT in small increments, and thus households may be less resistant to a higher VAT rate. But no conclusive evidence is currently available to support this hypothesis and it appears that the largest expansions in government spending in recent years have not been associated with any tax increases.

Table 1. Data About Value-Added Taxes of Selected European Countries

Country	Total Tax Revenue as a % of GDP at Market Prices (1998)[b]	General Consumption Taxes as a % of GDP (1998)	General Consumption Taxes as a % of Total Tax Revenues (1998)
Austria	44.4%	8.3%	18.7%
Belgium	45.9	7.0	15.3
Denmark	49.8	9.8	19.6
Finland	46.2	8.5	18.5
France	45.2	7.9	17.5
Germany	37.0	6.6	17.9
Greece[a]	33.7	7.7	22.9
Ireland	32.2	7.2	22.2
Italy	42.7	6.1	14.2
Luxembourg	41.5	5.7	13.7
Netherlands	41.0	6.9	16.9
Norway	43.6	9.3	21.3
Portugal	34.2	8.0	23.3
Spain	34.2	5.7	16.6
Sweden	52.0	7.1	13.6
United Kingdom	37.2	6.7	18.1

Sources: OECD, Paris, 2000.
a. Figures for Greece are for 1997.
b. GDP is an abbreviation for gross domestic product, which is a measure of total domestic output of goods and services.

LEGISLATION

H.R. 16 (Dingell)

National Health Insurance Act
Provides for a program of national health insurance. Imposes a value-added tax (VAT) to finance health benefits. Revenue from the VAT would initially be deposited into the proposed National Health Care Trust Fund. Introduced January 3, 2001; referred to the Committee on Ways and Means

and the Committee on Energy and Commerce. On February 7, 2001, this act was referred to the Subcommittee on Health of the Ways and Means Committee.

H.R. 86 (English)

Simplified USA Tax Act of 2001

Replaces the individual income tax, the corporate income tax, and the estate and gift taxes with a border-adjustable business tax (subtraction-method VAT) and a progressive consumed-income tax. Individuals may utilize the equivalent of universal Roth IRAs to encourage savings. Introduced January 3, 2001; referred to House Committee on Ways and Means.

H.R. 1040 (Armey)

Freedom and Fairness Restoration Act of 2001

(H.R. 1040 and S. 1040 are identical bills.) Repeals the corporate income tax, the individual income tax, and the estate tax and gift tax, and replaces these taxes with a flat rate consumption tax of 17%. Introduced March 15, 2001; referred to the Committee on Ways and Means and the Committee on Rules.

H.R. 2525 (Linder)

Fair Tax Act of 2001

Repeals the individual income tax, the corporate income tax, all payroll taxes, the self-employment tax, and the estate and gift taxes and levies a 23% national retail sales tax as a replacement. Every family would receive a rebate of the sales tax on spending up to the federal poverty level (plus an extra amount to prevent any marriage penalty). Introduced July 17, 2001; referred to the House Committee on Ways and Means.

H.R. 2717 (Tauzin)

Individual Tax Freedom Act of 2001

Effective July 1, 2003, levies a 15% national retail sales tax as a replacement for the individual and corporate income taxes, the estate and gift taxes, and certain excise taxes. This national retail sales tax would be administered primarily by the states. Introduced August 2, 2001; referred to the House Committee on Ways and Means and the House Rules Committee.

H.R. 4716 (DeMint)

Date Certain Tax Code Replacement Act

Establishes within the legislative branch a National Commission on Tax Reform and Simplification that shall review and and submit to Congress a report on (1) the present structure and provisions of the Internal Revenue Code; (2) whether tax systems imposed under the laws of other countries could provide more efficient, simple, and fair methods of funding the revenue requirements of the government; (3) whether the income tax should be replaced with a tax imposed in a different manner or on a different base; and (4) whether the Internal Revenue Code can be simplified, absent wholesale restructuring or replacement. Authorizes appropriations for the Commission. Any new federal tax system would require approval by Congress no later than July 4, 2005. If a new federal tax system is not approved by July 4, 2005, then Congress would be required to vote to reauthorize the Internal Revenue Code of 1986. Introduced May 14, 2002; referred to the House Committee on Ways and Means.

S. 1040 (Shelby)

Freedom and Fairness Restoration Act of 2001

(H.R. 1040 and S. 1040 are identical bills.) Repeals the corporate income tax, the individual income tax, and the estate and gift tax; and replaces these taxes with a flat rate consumption tax of 17%. Introduced June 14, 2001; referred to the Committee on Finance.

Chapter 4

VALUE-ADDED TAX IN CANADA: BACKGROUND, EVALUATION, AND IMPLICATIONS FOR THE UNITED STATES

SUMMARY

High forecasted U.S. budget deficits and the need for a revenue source to finance proposals for national health insurance have caused some Members of Congress to consider the feasibility of a U.S. value-added tax (VAT). A value-added tax is a tax, levied at each stage of production, on firms' value added. The value added of a firm is the difference between a firm's value of sales and a firm's purchases of inputs from other firms. A VAT is assumed to be fully shifted forward to consumers; hence, a VAT is a type of general consumption tax.

On January 1, 1991, Canada introduced a value-added tax, after protracted debate. An examination of the Canadian VAT may yield useful implications for a possible U.S. VAT. The Canadian economy and federal system of government have many similarities to those in the United States. Furthermore, the United States and Canada are each other's leading trading partners, and the two countries have a free trade agreement.

The Canadian VAT replaced its manufacturers' excise tax (named the federal sales tax or FST) primarily because of its inherent non-neutrality. The FST altered relative prices of goods which distorted household consumer choices by encouraging the substitution of untaxed goods for taxed goods.

The Canadian VAT has characteristics which approximate those of an optimal VAT, including a broad base, a single tax rate, and an income credit system to lessen regressivity. The major weakness was charging a zero-tax-rate on basic groceries.

Nine of the ten Canadian provinces have retail sales taxes (RSTs). Only the province of Quebec has agreed to tax the same goods and services under its RST as are taxed by the federal VAT. The other eight provinces have placed a greater value on their fiscal independence than on savings in administrative and compliance costs. But the Canadian VAT has co-existed with the retail sales taxes of the provinces.

Possible implications of the Canadian VAT for U.S. tax policy should not be overstated because there are important differences between the United States and Canada. In particular, the Canadian federal system of government is more decentralized than that of the United States, and the Canadian VAT was a replacement tax instead of a source of net new revenue.

BACKGROUND, EVALUATION, AND IMPLICATIONS FOR THE UNITED STATES

High forecasted U.S. budget deficits and the need for a revenue source to finance proposals for national health insurance have caused some Members of Congress to consider the feasibility of a U.S. value-added tax (VAT). A value–added tax is a tax, levied at each stage of production, on firms' value added. The value added of a firm is the difference between a firm's sales and a firm's purchases of inputs from other firms. In other words, a firm's value added is simply the amount of value a firm contributes to a good or service by applying its factors of production (land, labor, capital, and entrepreneurial ability). Another method of calculating a firm's value added is to total the firm's payments to its factors of production. A VAT is assumed to be fully shifted forward to consumers; hence, a VAT is a type of general consumption tax.

On January 1, 1991, Canada introduced a value-added tax. An examination of the Canadian VAT may yield useful implications for a possible U.S. VAT. The Canadian economy and federal system of government have many similarities to those in the United States. Furthermore, the United States and Canada are each other's leading trading partners, and the two countries have a free trade agreement.

Before discussing the possible implications of the Canadian VAT for the United States, this report describes the historical development of the Canadian VAT and evaluates its characteristics.

HISTORICAL DEVELOPMENT

The Canadian VAT replaced the Canadian manufacturers' excise tax which the Canadian Government called the federal sales tax (FST). In 1924, poor economic conditions caused the Canadian Government to levy an excise tax on manufactured goods. The FST was levied on a temporary basis, but a weak economy resulted in its continuation.

Attempts to Replace FST

From 1937 through 1982, major deficiencies of the FST resulted in numerous attempts to replace it with either a wholesale sales tax or a shared federal-province retail sales tax. In February 1983, the Federal Sales Tax Review Committee was established. A report from this Committee recommended that the FST be replaced with one of the following three taxes: a federal-provincial retail sales tax, a federal retail sales tax, or a federal value-added tax.[1]

In November 1984, the Canadian Government announced that it was considering levying a VAT. On June 17, 1987, the Minister of Finance published a White Paper concerning reforming the indirect tax system. The Minister proposed three possible replacements for both the FST and the provincial retail sales taxes.[2] These alternatives were a national retail sales tax, a goods and services tax (a VAT calculated by the credit-invoice method), and a business transfer tax (a VAT calculated by the subtraction method).[3] In March 1988, the Finance and Economic Affairs Committee, a House of Commons Standing Committee, published two reports about proposed broad-based consumption taxation. The first report recommended the broadest possible tax base (including home-consumed food) and a tax credit to reduce the tax burden on low-income families. The second report recommended that negotiations between the Canadian Government and the provincial governments be given high priority. On April 24, 1989, the Minister of Finance stated that the Canadian Government planned to levy a goods and services tax on January 1, 1991. On April 27, 1989, the budget

---

[1] Dominque, Richard. *Reform of the Federal Sales Tax: An Historical Perspective.* Library of Parliament. Mini Review no. 41 E, Ottawa, August 10, 1989. p. 2-4.
[2] Ibid., p. 4.
[3] The credit-invoice method and the subtraction method are described in the next section of this report.

gave some preliminary details, and on April 8, 1989, technical details were announced.[4]

Deficiencies of FST

The deficiencies of the FST which resulted in its eventual replacement can be placed into two categories: neutrality and complexity.

Non-neutralities of FST

In public finance, the more *neutral* a tax is, the less the tax affects private economic decisions, and consequently, the more efficient is the operation of the economy. The inherent non-neutrality of the FST was the primary reason for its eventual replacement by a VAT. The FST was non-neutral for both households and businesses.

For households, the FST altered relative prices of goods which distorted household consumer choices by encouraging the substitution of untaxed goods for taxed goods. There were five causes of this relative changes in prices. First, the FST only taxed manufactured goods. Consequently, manufactured goods rose in price relative to nonmanufactured goods. Second, diversity in distribution channels changed relative prices. Some manufacturers sold their products directly to wholesalers, others directly to retailers, and still others directly to consumers.[5] The more stages of distribution between the manufacturer and the consumer, the smaller the FST as a percentage of the consumer price, all other things being equal. Third, variations in distribution margins across goods changed relative prices. The greater was the percentage mark-up at the wholesale and retail levels, the smaller was the FST as a percent of the consumer price, all other things being equal. Fourth, domestic manufactured goods tended to include more distribution costs than imported manufactured goods at the point of imposition of the tax; and consequently, domestic manufactured goods were taxed more heavily by the FST. These distribution costs included advertising, warranty, and favorable terms on trade credit to distributors.[6]

For firms, the FST was not fully excluded from producers' goods, that is, from man-made goods used in the production process. As a percentage of sales, some firms paid more FST on intermediate inputs and capital goods

---

[4] Dominque, Richard. *Reform of the Federal Sales Tax: An Historical Perspective*, p. 3-5.
[5] Gillis, Malcolm. Excising Excises: Federal Sales Tax Reform in Canada in *Report of Proceedings of the Thirty-Sixth Conference*. Canadian Tax Foundation. 1984. p. 466-467.
[6] Ibid., p. 467-468.

than other firms; consequently, the relative prices of goods to consumers were altered. Exporters were hurt by paying FST on producers' goods.[7]

Complexities of FST

Critics of the Canadian FST argued that its complexity raised administrative and compliance costs. Although only 75,000 firms collected the FST, the tax had 22,000 special provisions and administrative arrangements. The FST became a target of firms attempting to obtain preferential tax treatment for their goods.[8] The standard tax rate was 13.5 percent, but numerous goods were taxed at other rates. Compliance difficulties include[d] problems arising from the lack of formal appeal procedures, secrecy in rulings, and the ongoing attempts, through notional valuations, to equalize the burden borne by competing products sold through different distribution channels. Efforts to rectify the inherent shortcomings of the tax, then, often result[ed] in the trading of one set of administrative-compliance difficulties for another.[9]

Thus, the potentially low administrative and compliance costs of the FST had not been realized.

Replacement of FST with a VAT

Despite its deficiencies, the FST continued from 1924 to January 1, 1991. The Canadian Government had great difficulty in replacing it primarily because of its hidden nature. In 1989, the FST amounted to $18 billion (Canadian dollars) or more than $700 per capita. But consumers never saw the tax listed on any retail sales receipts; consequently, consumers arguably felt that most, if not all, of the burden of the FST was levied on business owners.

The Canadian Government maintained that taxes should be explicit in order for the government to be accountable for any tax increases. The Canadian Government argued that the hidden nature of the FST was a deficiency.[10] Hence, the Canadian Government designed its VAT with the requirement that for each taxable sale either the sales receipt would show the amount of the tax or an in-store sign would clearly state that a 7-percent

---

[7] Ibid., p. 466.
[8] *Goods and Services Tax: A Summary*. Department of Finance. Ottawa, October 1990. p. 7.
[9] Gillis, p. 471.
[10] *Goods and Services Tax: A Summary*, p. 8.

VAT was included in the price.[11] The Canadian Government labeled its VAT as a goods and services tax or GST.

The shift from a hidden FST to a deliberately visible VAT resulted in substantial public opposition. Nevertheless, the Canadian Government approved the GST after much deliberation and debate. Because the VAT had been operational in other countries since 1967 and because most developed nations had VATs, the Canadian Government had the advantage of obtaining information from tax experts in order to avoid mistakes and pitfall in designing its VAT.

The replacement of the FST with a VAT was the primary component of a tax-reform package. The package also included an increase in the existing high-income surtax on personal income and an increase in the income credit for broad-based consumption taxes paid.[12]

EVALUATION OF THE CANADIAN VAT

In order to evaluation the Canadian VAT, descriptions of the characteristics of an optimal VAT are warranted. Then, the characteristics of the Canadian VAT may be compared with the characteristics of an optimal VAT. Finally, the intergovernmental aspects of the Canadian VAT can be examined.

Characteristics of an Optimal VAT

Tax economists agree that an optimal VAT should have five characteristics.

- It should be a consumption type VAT
- The method of calculating the VAT should be designed for ease of computation and administration.
- It should have a broad base.
- It should have a single tax rate.
- The preferred method for reducing the regressivity of the VAT is some form of an income-credit system.

---

[11] Ibid., p. 11.
[12] Grady, Patrick. An Analysis of the Distributional Impact of the Goods and Services Tax. *Canadian Tax Journal*, v. 38, no. 3, May/June 1990. p. 635.

These five characteristics are examined in the following sections.[13] Then, the next section compares the actual characteristics of the Canadian VAT with those of an optimal VAT.

Types of VAT

There are three types of VATs which differ in their tax treatment of purchases of capital inputs (plant and equipment). Under the *consumption VAT*, capital purchases are treated the same way as the purchase of any other input. This tax treatment of capital purchases is equivalent to expensing which makes the payment of the tax come from consumer expenditures. Under the *income VAT*, the VAT paid on the purchases of capital inputs is amortized (credited against the firm's VAT liability) over the expected lives of the capital inputs which puts the payment of the tax on factor incomes. Under the *gross product VAT*, no deduction for the VAT on purchases of capital inputs is allowed against the firm's VAT liability which causes the tax to fall on capital.

Before Canada levied its VAT, all 20 nations in the Organization of Economic Co-operation and Development (OECD) with VATs used the consumption type.[14] Indeed, most VAT advocates intend to shift tax burdens from capital income to consumption; and if the desire is to tax incomes, there are better ways to do so.

Methods of Calculating VAT

There are three alternative methods of calculating VAT: the credit method, the subtraction method, and the addition method. Under the *credit method*, a firm would calculate the VAT to be remitted to the Government by a two–step process. First, the firm would multiply its sales by the tax rate to calculate VAT collected on sales. Second, the firm would credit VAT paid on inputs against VAT collected on sales and remit this difference to the Government. Under the *credit–invoice method*, a type of credit method, the firm is required to show VAT separately on all sales invoices and to calculate the VAT credit on inputs by adding all VAT shown on purchase invoices.

Under the *subtraction method*, the firm would calculate its value added by subtracting its cost of taxed inputs from its sales. Next, the firm would

---

[13] For more detailed explanations of these five characteristics, see: Bickley, James M. *Value-Added Tax: Concepts, Policy Issues, and OECD Experiences*. Report No. 92-938 E. Washington, Congressional Research Service, 1992. 49 p.

[14] The OECD is an international governmental body dedicated to promoting international trade, economic growth, and economic stability. The OECD consists of 18 European nations, Turkey, the United States, Canada, Australia, New Zealand, and Japan.

determine its VAT liability by multiplying its value added by the VAT rate. Under the *addition method*, the firm would calculate its value added by adding all payments for untaxed inputs (e.g. wages and profits). Next, the firm would multiply its value added by the VAT rate to calculate VAT to be remitted to the Government.

Before the imposition of the Canadian VAT, the credit–invoice method was used by all 20 OECD nations with VATs. The credit–invoice method requires registered firms to maintain detailed records that are cross indexed with supporting documentation. A VAT shown on the sales invoice of one firm is the same as the VAT shown on the purchase order of another firm. Hence, the credit–invoice method allows tax auditors to cross check the records of firms. Also, each firm has a vested interest in insuring that the VAT shown on their purchase orders is not understated in order that the firm receive full credit against VAT liability for VAT previously paid. Thus, the credit-invoice method is generally thought by tax administrators to be easier to enforce. The credit–invoice method is probably the only feasible method if there are to be multiple tax rates.

VAT Base

The potential revenue from a VAT would vary with the comprehensiveness of the tax base. A broad–based VAT would have limited exclusions, while a narrow–based VAT would have numerous exclusions. Obviously, the broader the tax base, the lower the tax rate necessary to raise a given amount of revenue.

Furthermore, the broader the VAT base, the more efficient is the tax system. The exclusion of goods from taxation changes their prices relative to taxed goods. Changes in relative prices cause economic distortions. Consumers tend to substitute lower priced goods for higher priced goods.

No VAT proposal would tax all goods. The two fundamental methods of giving special tax treatment to a good are exemption and zero–rating. A business producing an exempt good would not collect VAT on its sales and would not receive credit for VAT paid on its purchases of inputs. This business would not register with tax authorities and, consequently, would not be part of the VAT system. Hence, a business producing an exempt good would not have the usual VAT compliance costs and would not impose administrative costs on the Government (except verification of its exemption, of course). This business's costs, however, include any tax paid on inputs, because it receives no credit for previously paid taxes. The exemption of a good at a pre-retail stage of production would cause the VAT to cascade, that is, VAT would be charged of previously paid VAT.

A business producing a zero-rated good would not collect VAT on its sales but would receive credit for VAT paid on its inputs. This is equivalent to the business being charged a zero-tax-rate on the goods it produces. This business would be a registered taxpayer and, consequently, would involve the usual compliance and administrative costs. A business producing a zero–rated good, however, would receive a refund of any VAT paid on its inputs; therefore, its costs would not include VAT paid at earlier stages. The effects on final prices and total VAT collected by the Government caused by exempting or zero–rating goods would vary with the stage of production.

Single Rate

Tax economists recommend a single VAT tax rate in order to make the VAT more neutral and to reduce administrative and compliance costs.[15] Multiple rates encourage consumers to purchase more of the goods with lower tax rates and fewer with higher tax rates. Thus multiple tax rates alter relative prices which distorts consumer choices and, consequently, reduces consumer well-being.

Multiple rates require auditors to determine if goods are classified in the proper category. One common method of evasion used by a firm is to falsely classify goods into a category with a lower tax rate. Multiple rates make numerous calculations by public administrators more complex. Finally, multiple rates increase firms' costs of complying with a VAT. A firm must place goods in different rate categories and make more tax calculations.

Income Credit System

If disposable income over a one-year period is the measure of ability–to–pay, then a VAT would be viewed as extremely regressive; that is, the percentage of disposable income paid in VAT would decrease rapidly as disposable income increases. In most discussions of tax policy, both a one–year period and annual disposable income (or some other annual income measure) are used; consequently, the VAT is viewed as being extremely regressive.

Some supporters of progressive taxation oppose the VAT primarily because they believe that it is regressive. Some of these critics are especially concerned about the absolute burden of a VAT on low-income households. The degree of regressivity, however, can be reduced by government policy. Three often–mentioned policies are: exclusions and multiple rates, income

---

[15] For a comprehensive presentation of the advantages of a single tax rate, see: Cnossen, Sijbren. What Rate Structure for a Goods and Services Tax? The European Experience. *Canadian Tax Journal*, v. 37, no. 5, September/October 1989. p. 1,167–1,181.

tax credits, and earmarking of some revenues for increased social spending (including indexed transfer payments).

Tax economists generally oppose *exclusions and multiple rates* to reduce regressivity for four reasons. First, exclusions and multiple rates increase administrative and compliance costs. Second, exclusions and multiple rates distort relative prices which reduces tax neutrality. In addition, if a VAT is to raise a given amount of revenue, then revenue lost from excluding goods must be offset by higher VAT rates. These higher rates increase the distortion in relative prices and, consequently, further reduce the neutrality of the tax system. Third, the possible reduction in regressivity from exclusion and multiple rates is declining because consumption patterns for different income levels are becoming more similar.[16] Fourth, for a one-year time period, the reduction in regressivity is small, particularly for low-income households.

A second option to reduce or eliminate regressivity is to *earmark some of the VAT revenue* to finance an increase in income-tested transfers. For example, in the United States, benefits for the food stamp program could be increased. But this approach would not always assist the working poor.

As a third option, an *income-credit system* with either a flat credit or a credit that diminishes as income rises could be established. This credit method could be operated in two different ways. First, an individual could apply the credit against his income tax liability and thus lower his liability on a dollar–for–dollar basis. If the tax credit exceeded the individual's tax liability, he could apply for a refund of the excess credit. A taxpayer already due a tax refund could increase the size of his refund by the amount of the tax credit. A household not subject to income taxation could apply for a tax refund equal to the credit. An income tax credit that declines as income increases could reduce regressivity more sharply than a flat income tax credit.

Alternatively, a stand–alone credit system could be established which would not require an eligible household to file an income tax return in order to obtain a refund for VAT paid. An eligible household would have to submit a simple form in order to receive a refund. A stand–alone credit system may be more effective than the income tax credit in encouraging low-income households to file for a refund, but administrative and compliance costs would be higher because a new system would have to be established.

---

[16] Cnossen, p. 1,175.

If the regressivity of a VAT is to be reduced, tax experts prefer some form of an income-credit system. Assistance could be targeted towards the poor with reasonable administrative and compliance costs.

Optimal VAT versus Canadian VAT

The five characteristics of an optimal VAT may be compared with these five characteristics of the Canadian VAT. First, the Canadian VAT is the consumption type. Second, the Canadian VAT is calculated by using the credit method but not the credit-invoice method. Sellers are not required to issue invoices. "Sellers must attest to their purchasers that their GST liability has been paid, and they must retain records of taxes paid on purchases to be eligible for a credit."[17] Because invoices are not required, sellers are able to save on compliance costs, but the government has greater difficulty enforcing VAT compliance.

Third, the Canadian VAT has a broad VAT base compared to most VATs because it zero-rates or exempts few products. The major exception is the zero-rating of "basic groceries (most foods intended to prepared and consumed at home)."[18] The taxation of home-consumed food is difficult politically. Most developed nations tax home-consumed food at a reduced rate. But, the zero-rating of home-consumed food increases compliance and administrative costs. A major tax complexity is caused by separating tax-free food items from taxable food items. The Canadian Government used the same definition for basis groceries that had been applied under its FST (manufacturers' excise tax). For example, the VAT is levied on milk, fruit juices (large containers), bread, cakes and pies (full size), and other baked goods when sold in quantities of six or more.[19] But, the VAT is not levied on soft drinks, drinks dispensed in a store, snack foods, sandwiches and prepared salads, single-serving baked goods sold in quantities of fewer than six, and single-serving containers of yogurt, puddings and drinks other than plain milk.[20]

The Canadian VAT also zero-rates prescription drugs and medical devices. The Canadian VAT exempts residential rents, resales of existing

---

[17] Tax Executives Institute. *Value-Added Taxes: A Comparative Analysis*. Washington, 1992. p. 78.
[18] *Goods and Services Tax: A Summary*, p. 13.
[19] Ibid., p. 17.
[20] Ibid.

houses, most health and dental services, financial services, day-care services, municipal transit, and most educational services.[21]

Fourth, the Canadian VAT has a single rate (seven percent) rather than multiple rates. Fifth, the Canadian VAT relies *primarily* on an income-credit system to reduce the regressivity of its VAT, as recommended by tax economists. The Canadian VAT expanded the existing refundable sales tax credit used for its FST.

The VAT credit against income is calculated annually and paid in quarterly installments. The credit is paid to all families and individuals whose previous-year incomes fell below minimum income levels. The amount of the credit people receive increases as their family's size rises and their family income declines. For 1991, a single person with a income of up to $30,000 (Canadian) received a credit, and a couple with two children with income of up to $36,000 (Canadian) received a credit. The income thresholds for the credit are indexed for inflation.[22]

As previously discussed, the Canadian VAT zero-rates basic groceries in order to lessen the regressivity of the VAT. But this reduction in regressivity from zero-rating food is limited because the zero-rate is based on a category of purchase, not the amount spent, and higher income families purchase more expensive foods.

In conclusion, the Canadian VAT has characteristics which approximate those of an optimal VAT.

Intergovernmental Relations

Between 1937 and 1967, nine of the ten Canadian provinces permanently levied a retail sales tax (RST). The provinces opposed the Canadian VAT because of concern that the Canadian Government was encroaching of their retail sales tax base.[23]

The Canadian Government had hoped that the provinces would adopt the VAT base for their retail sales taxes and agree to jointly collect both taxes. Despite large potential savings in administrative and compliance costs, only Quebec has adopted the same tax base.[24] All costs of administration are split on a 50/50 basis. Quebec is responsible for the day-to-day

---

[21] *The National Finances, 1992.* Canadian Tax Foundation. Toronto, 1992. Chapter 8, p. 3.
[22] *Goods and Services Tax: A Summary*, p. 13-15.
[23] Dominque, Richard. *The Goods and Services Tax: Provincial Perspective.* Library of Parliament. Backgrounder no. BP-210 E, Ottawa, November 1989. p. 3.
[24] Tax Executives Institute. *Value-Added Taxes: A Comparative Analysis*, p. 102.

administrative functions of the VAT, but the Canadian Government continues to be solely responsible for VAT legislation and policy matters to ensure that the VAT is applied uniformly across the nation.[25] The other eight provinces with retail sales taxes do not want to lose their flexibility and control in setting their tax policies. The retail sales taxes of these eight provinces have continued to co-exist with the Canadian VAT.

IMPLICATIONS FOR THE UNITED STATES

The Canadian VAT is important for the United States because Canada and the United States are each other's leading trading partner, and the two countries have a free trade agreement. Canada has a federal system of government and is the most recent developed nation to implement a VAT. The United States and Canada have similar standards of living. Consequently, the Canadian VAT has four possible implications for U.S. tax policy.

First, the Canadian VAT was controversial and was approved only after protracted debate in the legislature. During the past two U.S. Congresses, six bills proposing a VAT were introduced. Currently, there is widespread congressional examination of the VAT.

Second, the Canadian VAT ultimately approved was close to an optimal VAT, according to standards of tax economists. The major weakness was the zero-rating of basic groceries. The two other most recent VATs levied by OECD members (Japan and New Zealand) also were close to optimal.

Third, except for Quebec, no province has adopted the VAT base. The provinces have placed a greater value on their fiscal independence than on savings in administrative and compliance costs. Hence, if a Federal VAT is approved in the United States, those States with retail sales taxes may not adopt the Federal VAT base for their RSTs.

Fourth, the Canadian VAT has co-existed with the retail sales taxes of the provinces. For the United States, this suggests that State RSTs could coexist with a Federal VAT.

These possible implications for the United States should not be overstated because there are important differences between the United States and Canada. In particular, the Canadian federal system of government is more decentralized than that of the United States, and the Canadian VAT was a replacement tax instead of a source of net new revenue.

---

[25] Ibid.

Selected Bibliography

Cnossen, Sijbren. What rate structure for a goods and services tax? The European experience. Canadian tax journal, v. 37, no. 5, September/October 1989: 1,167-1,181.

Dominque, Richard. Reform of the federal sales tax: an historical perspective. Library of Parliament. Mini review no. 41 E, Ottawa, August 10, 1989. 6 p.

----- The goods and services tax: provincial perspective. Library of Parliament. Backgrounder no. BP-210 E, Ottawa, November 1989. 19 p.

Gillis, Malcolm. Excising excises: federal sales tax reform in Canada. Report of proceedings of the thirty-sixth conference. Canadian Tax Foundation, 1984: 460-476.

Goods and services tax: a summary. Department of Finance. Ottawa, October 1990. 102 p.

Grady, Patrick. An analysis of the distributional impact of the goods and services tax. Canadian tax journal, v. 38, no. 3, May/June 1990: 632-643.

Tax Executives Institute. Value-added taxes: a comparative analysis. Washington, 1992. 140 p.

The national finances, 1992. Canadian Tax Foundation. Toronto, 1992. 352 p.

U.S. Library of Congress. Congressional Research Service. Value-added tax: concepts, policy issues, and OECD experiences, by James M. Bickley. [Washington] December 11, 1992. 49 p.

Chapter 5

VALUE-ADDED TAX: REVENUE ESTIMATES

SUMMARY

Large current and projected deficits in the Federal budget and proposals for national health insurance have caused Congress to consider new sources of revenue, including a value-added tax (VAT). Furthermore, there have been proposals to use the revenue from a VAT to replace a portion of the revenue from taxes on income. A VAT is a multistage consumption tax levied on each firm's value added, that is, the difference between each firm's sales and its purchases from other firms.

The potential revenue from a VAT would vary with the comprehensiveness of the tax base. A broad-based VAT would have limited exclusions, while a narrow-based VAT would have numerous exclusions. Obviously, the broader the base, the lower the tax rate necessary to raise a given amount of revenue.

The estimated revenue from a VAT would be different if the VAT is a *new source of revenue* rather than a *replacement tax*. If the VAT is a new revenue source, its gross revenue would be partially offset by reductions in revenues from personal income taxes, corporate income taxes, and social security taxes. Based on estimating conventions and tax calculations by the Congressional Budget Office, CRS chose to assume that the reduction in taxes on income *offset 25 percent* of the revenue of the new tax. For fiscal year 1995, it is estimated that, for each 1-percent levied, a broad-based VAT would generate *net* revenue between $26.5 billion and $27.7 billion as a new revenue source. Also, for fiscal year 1995, a narrow–based VAT, for each 1–percent levied, would generate *net* revenue between $13.8 billion and $16.7 billion as a new revenue source.

The estimated *net* revenue from a VAT as a replacement tax would vary dramatically depending on the tax replaced. Since the VAT is an indirect business tax, if the revenue from a VAT replaces the revenue from some other *indirect business tax* (that is, excise taxes, customs duties, and miscellaneous receipts), then each dollar of VAT revenue would replace a dollar of revenue of another indirect tax. The revenue from a VAT could be used to replace the revenue from a *direct tax* (that is, individual income tax, corporate income tax, or payroll tax). But more than one dollar of gross VAT revenue would be needed to replace each dollar of a direct tax because the VAT would reduce factor incomes, and, thus, revenue from direct taxes.

These revenue estimates should be considered as approximations. The actual revenue yields could vary depending on the complexity and structure of the VAT.

INTRODUCTION

Large current and projected deficits in the Federal budget and proposals for national health insurance have sparked congressional interest in possible sources of additional revenue including a value–added tax (VAT).[1] Furthermore, there have been proposals to use the revenue from a VAT to replace revenue from other taxes. The value added of a firm is the difference between that firm's sales and its purchases from other firms. A VAT is levied on firms' value added at all stages of production. In order to narrow the scope of this report, it is assumed that the VAT is the consumption–type which has been adopted by all European nations with VATs. A consumption VAT treats all purchases, including capital purchases, as deductible in calculating a firm's value added. The consumption VAT base, therefore, is the value–added included in consumer products, which is the same as their retail price. Hence, a consumption VAT does not tax capital and simplifies the calculation of value added.

The nearly universal method of calculating VAT is the credit–invoice method which requires each firm to show VAT separately on all sales invoices. Each sale would be marked up by the amount of the VAT. A sales

---

[1] For a concise discussion of imposing a VAT as a new revenue source, see: U.S. Library of Congress. Congressional Research Service. *Value–Added Tax as a New Revenue Source.* Issue Brief No. 91078, by James M. Bickley. [Washington] 1991. (Updated regularly).

invoice for a seller is a purchase invoice for a buyer. A firm would calculate the VAT to be remitted to the Government by a simple three-step process. First, the firm would aggregate VAT shown on its sales invoices. Second, the firm would aggregate VAT shown on its purchase invoices. Finally, aggregate VAT on purchase invoices would be subtracted from aggregate VAT shown on sales invoices and the difference remitted to the Government. If aggregate VAT paid on purchase invoices exceed aggregate VAT shown on sales invoices, then the firm would receive a rebate of the difference from the Government. In this report, it is assumed that firms calculate VAT to be remitted to the Government by using the credit–invoice method.

A revenue estimating convention, which permits revenues to be measured in constant dollars, assumes that a VAT would not change the amount of gross domestic product (GDP) or the aggregate price level. Under the convention, ignoring any cyclical effect, if the money supply is not increased, GDP is not increased and the VAT must be shifted backward and reduce factor incomes which would reduce revenues from the personal income tax, the corporate income tax, and social security taxes. Based on the estimating convention used by the Congressional Budget Office (CBO), CRS chose to use a revenue offset of 25 percent, that is, declines in taxes on income would offset 25 percent of the revenue from the new tax. Hence, if a VAT is a new revenue source, net VAT revenue would equal 75 percent of gross VAT revenue.[2]

For example, assume a VAT has gross revenues of $100 billion. The payment of $100 billion of VAT reduces wages and capital income by $100 billion; consequently, individual income tax revenue declines by $18 billion, payroll tax revenue declines by $5 billion, and corporate income tax revenue declines by $2 billion. Thus, net revenue from the VAT equals $75 billion; that is, $100 billion less $25 billion ($18 billion plus $5 billion plus $2 billion).[3]

---

[2] For an explanation of estimating convention including revenue offsets, see: U.S. Congress. Joint Committee on Taxation. *Discussion of Revenue Estimation Methodology and Process*. Washington, U.S. Govt. Print. Off., 1992. 22 p.

[3] In the national income accounts, gross domestic produce (GDP) less depreciation equal net national product (NNP). Net national product less indirect business taxes (IBT) equals national income (NI). A VAT is a form of indirect business tax. Hence, a VAT would reduce NI which in turn would lower revenue from taxes on income.

VAT BASE

The potential revenue per 1-percent rate from a VAT would vary with the comprehensiveness of the tax base. The two fundamental methods of giving special VAT treatment to businesses in an industry are exemption and zero-rating. An *exempt* business would not collect VAT on its sales and would not receive credit for VAT paid on its purchases of inputs. An exempt business would not register with tax authorities.

A *zero-rated* business would not collect VAT on its sales but would receive credit for VAT paid on its inputs. This is equivalent to the business being charged a zero tax rate. A zero-rated business would be a registered taxpayer, and consequently, would involve the usual compliance and administrative costs. A zero-rated business, however, receives a refund of any VAT paid on its inputs, so its costs do not include VAT paid at earlier stages. The effects on final prices and total VAT collected by the Government caused by exempting or zero-rating firms would vary with the stage of production.

A zero-rated retailer would not charge any VAT on its sales, but it would receive credit for all VAT previously paid on inputs. A zero-rated retailer would not remit VAT to the Government, but it would receive a refund for VAT previously paid by suppliers. Hence, the price of the commodity would not include any VAT, and the Government would receive no revenue. For this report, the simplifying assumption is made that all items excluded from taxation are zero-rated at the retail stage.

A broad-based VAT would have limited exclusions, while a narrow-based VAT would have numerous exclusions. Obviously, the broader the tax base, the lower the tax rate necessary to raise a given amount of revenue. Furthermore, the broader the VAT base, the more efficient is the tax system. The exclusion of commodities from taxation changes their prices relative to taxed commodities. Changes in relative prices cause economic distortions. Consumers tend to substitute lower priced commodities for higher priced commodities.

There are three primary justifications for excluding specific items from taxation.[4] First, the VAT would be difficult to collect because some sellers of goods and services could easily avoid reporting their sales. For example, VAT would be difficult to collect on expenditures for domestic services and

---

[4] This classification of justifications for exclusion from VAT taxation was derived from the following source: Tait, Alan A. *Value-Added Tax: International Practice and Problems.* International Monetary Fund, Washington, 1988. p. 56.

expenditures abroad by U.S. residents. Second, some items are excluded on equity grounds, since these items claim disproportionately large percentages of the incomes of lower income families.[5] Third, some goods may be excluded because they are merit goods, that is, "goods the provision of which society (as distinct from the preferences of the individual consumer) wishes to encourage..."[6] Some items may be justified for exclusion for more than one reason.

For this report, two well-known formulations of broad and narrow tax bases for a VAT were updated using current data. A third set of VAT bases was formulated by CRS as a means of evaluating the other bases. These VAT bases are used in the next section to estimate the revenue from a VAT.

In the first source, Professor Charles E. McLure constructed broad and narrow tax bases for a consumption value–added tax using 1984 Department of Commerce data. CRS used 1991 Department of Commerce data to update McLure's calculations. McLure used his own judgment in determining which items to exclude in order to establish a broad–based and narrow–based VAT. His broad–based VAT would have limited exemptions, and his narrow–based VAT would have liberal exemptions, as shown in table 1. McLure's broad–based and narrow–based VATs would be levied on 76.3 percent and 44.8 percent of personal consumption expenditures, respectively.[7]

In the second source, Professors Richard and Peggy Musgrave examined exclusions from State sales taxes using Department of Commerce data for 1981. CRS used 1991 Department of Commerce data to update the Musgraves' calculations. A consumption VAT and a national sales tax (NST) have conceptually the same tax base; consequently, the Musgraves' calculations can be used in estimating revenues from a VAT. The Musgraves derived a broad–based NST by calculating the percentage of personal consumption *generally* excluded from State sales taxation. Examples of *generally* excluded items are food furnished to employees, insurance premiums, and foreign travel. *Generally* excluded items reduced the tax base to 73.9 percent of consumer expenditures.[8]

---

[5] The regressivity of the VAT would be only slightly reduced by zero–rating necessities such as food, housing, and utilities. For data that demonstrates this slight reduction in regressivity, see: U.S. Congressional Budget Office. *Effects of Adopting a Value–Added Tax.* Washington, February 1992. p. 34–37.

[6] Musgrave, Richard A., and Peggy B. Musgrave. *Public Finance in Theory and Practice.* 4th ed. New York, McGraw–Hill, 1984. p. 78.

[7] McLure, Charles E. *The Value–Added Tax: Key to Deficit Reduction.* American Enterprise Institute, Washington, D.C., 1987. p. 20–23.

[8] Musgrave, p. 437–438.

Furthermore, the Musgraves identified items which were *frequently* excluded from State sales taxes. Examples of *frequently* excluded items are home–consumed food, household utilities, and private education. They derived a narrow–based NST by excluding items that are either *generally* or *frequently* excluded from State sales taxation. This narrow–based NST would be imposed on 38.4 percent of consumer expenditures.[9] All items *generally* or *frequently* excluded from State sales taxation are listed in table 2.

Both of these formulations of VAT bases have some problems in the choice of exactly which items might be taxed; obviously, many of these decisions about a real–world VAT are subjective. Table 3 presents another selection of consumer expenditure items, based on a review of the literature. In these alternative formulations, a broad–based VAT would be based on about 77 percent of consumer expenditures and a narrow–based one would cover about 47 percent.

The remarkable thing about all these bases is how close the total maximum and minimum tax bases actually are, despite the differences in the items chosen for exclusion. This suggests that the revenue estimates presented in the next section are reasonable approximations of the maximum and minimum revenues that might be expected from a 1–percent value–added tax.

CALCULATION OF REVENUE ESTIMATES

Data Resources, Inc. (DRI) forecasts that total personal consumption expenditures will be $4,781.8 billion in current dollars for fiscal year 1995 (October 1, 1994 — September 30, 1995).[10] This aggregate level of personal consumption expenditures and the tax bases formulated by McLure, the Musgraves, and CRS may be used to estimate revenue per 1–percent VAT.

The revenue estimates would vary depending on whether or not the VAT would be a new revenue source or a replacement for another tax (and which tax it replaces). Furthermore, revenue estimates would vary with the broadness of the base.

---

[9] Ibid.
[10] Data Resources, Inc. *Review of the U.S. Economy*, May 1993. p. 9.

Table 1. Estimated Base of Consumption–Based Value–Added Tax with Limited and Liberal Exclusions, at 1991 Levels of Consumption (billions of dollars)

	Personal Consumption Expenditures	Estimated Tax Base	
		Limited Exclusions	Liberal Exclusions
Food and tobacco	665.4	653.6[a]	246.3[b]
Clothing, accessories, and jewelry	260.6	260.4[c]	260.4[c]
Personal care	62.2	62.2	62.2
Housing	574.0	163.1[d]	–
Household operation	441.7	431.8[e]	288.6[f]
Medical care expenses	656.0	507.9[g]	–
Personal business	317.7	130.6[h]	130.6[h]
Transportation	438.2	438.2	430.5[i]
Recreation	289.7	289.7	281.0[j]
Private education and research	92.8	–	–
Religious and welfare activities	107.7	–	–
Foreign travel and other, net	+18.3	58.1[k]	58.1[k]
Total personal consumption	3,924.3	2,995.6	1,757.7
Percentage of personal consumption	100.0%	76.3%	44.8%

[a] Excludes food furnished to government and commercial employees and food produced and consumed on farms.
[b] Includes only purchased meals, beverages, and tobacco products.
[c] Excludes standard clothing issued to military personnel.
[d] Includes only purchases of new houses.
[e] Excludes domestic services.
[f] Excludes domestic services and household utilities except telephone.
[g] Excludes physicians' services.
[h] Excludes services furnished without payment by financial intermediaries except life insurance companies and expenses of handling life insurance.
[i] Excludes bridge, tunnel, ferry, and road tolls; and mass transit systems.
[j] Excludes clubs and fraternal organizations.
[k] Excludes foreign travel and expenditures abroad by U.S. residents but includes expenditures in United States by foreigners.
Table updated from McLure, Charles E. *The Value–Added Tax: Key to Deficit Reduction.* American Enterprise Institute, Washington, DC, 1987. p. 21.
Source: U.S. Department of Commerce, *Survey of Current Business* (July 1992). p. 59, 78.

Table2. Estimated Base of a Value–Added Tax, 1991 (billions of dollars)

Total consumer expenditures	$3,924.3
Items generally excluded:	
Housing[a]	574.0
Domestic services	9.9
Food furnished employees	11.3
Medical supplies[b]	75.9
Foreign travel	36.1
Other personal business	317.7
Remaining base	2,899.4
As percentage of total consumption	73.9%
Items frequently excluded:	
Home–consumed food	$407.4
Other medical expenses[c]	489.3
Household utilities	143.2
Tobacco	47.8
Gasoline	105.5
Private education	92.8
Religious and welfare activities	107.7
Remaining base	1,505.7
As percentage of total consumption:	38.4%

[a] Includes rental payments and imputed rent of owner–occupied housing.
[b] Includes ophthalmic products, orthopedic appliances, drug preparations, and sundries.
[c] Includes services of medical personnel, current expenditures of nonprofit medical institutions, payments by patients of proprietary medical institutions, and health insurance.

Table updated from Musgrave, Richard A., and Peggy B. Musgrave. *Public Finance in Theory and Practice*. 4th ed. New York, McGraw–Hill, 1984. p. 437.

Source of data: U.S. Department of Commerce. *Survey of Current Business*, July 1992. p. 59, 78.

Table 3. Alternative Bases for a Value–Added Tax, 1991 (billions of dollars)

Total consumer expenditures		$3,924.3
Expenditures excluded from a broad–based VAT:		
Food furnished employees (including military)		11.3
Food produced and consumed on farms		0.5
Standard clothing issued to military personnel		0.2
Net taxable housing:		
Rental value of housing	574.0	
less: expenditures for new housing	163.1	
		410.9
Domestic service		9.9
Health insurance		38.3
Service furnished without payment by financial intermediaries[a]		127.4
Expense of handling life insurance		59.7
Net purchases of used autos		35.8
Auto insurance premiums less claims paid		21.8
Private education and research		92.8
Religious and welfare activities		107.7
Foreign travel and other, net		
Foreign travel by U.S. residents	36.2	
plus: expenditures abroad by U.S. residents	4.2	
less: expenditures in the U.S. by nonresidents	58.1	
less: personal remittances in kind to nonresidents	0.6	
		-18.3
Total exclusions		898.0
Broad VAT base		3,026.3
As percentage of total consumption		77.1%
Additional expenditures excluded from a narrow VAT base:		
Food purchased for off–premise consumption		407.4
Expenditures for new housing		163.1
Medical care (other than health insurance)		617.7
Clubs and fraternal organizations except insurance		8.7
Total additional exclusions		1,196.9
Narrow VAT base		1,829.4
As percentage of total consumption		46.6%

[a]Except life insurance carriers and private uninsured pension plans.
Source of data: U.S. Department of Commerce. *Survey of Current Business*, July 1992. p. 59, 78.

New Revenue Source

For FY95, table 4 shows gross and net revenue estimates per one–percent VAT for the tax bases formulated by McLure, the Musgraves, and CRS if the VAT is a new revenue source. As previously indicated, if a VAT is a new revenue source, the estimated net VAT revenue for legislative purposes would equal 75 percent of gross VAT revenue because declines in taxes on income would offset 25 percent of gross VAT revenue. Consistent with the way CBO would adjust its baseline after enactment, this 25 percent offset would consist of individual income tax revenue (18 percent), payroll tax revenue (5 percent), and corporate income tax revenue (2 percent).

For FY95, based on McLure's work, it is estimated that a 1–percent VAT with a broad base would raise *gross* revenue of $36.5 billion (.01 × .763 × $4,781.8 billion) and *net* revenue of $27.4 billion (.01 × .763 × $4,781.8 × .75). A 1–percent VAT, with a narrow base, according to McLure's work, would raise *net* revenue of an estimated $16.1 billion.

For FY95, a 1–percent VAT as a new revenue source, based on the Musgraves' work, would raise *net* revenue of approximately $26.5 billion with a broad base and $13.8 billion with a narrow base. For FY95, the tax bases formulated in table 3 would result in similar revenue estimates compared to the preceding estimates derived from work done by McLure and the Musgraves. It is estimated that a 1–percent VAT would raise *net* revenue of $27.7 billion with a broad base and $16.7 billion with a narrow base.

TABLE 4. Estimated Revenue from a Value–Added Tax if a New Revenue Source, FY95

Source of Base	Type of Base	Estimated Percentage of Personal Consumption	Revenue Per One–Percent Tax FY95 (billions of dollars)	
			Gross Revenue	Net Revenue
McLure	Broad	76.3%	$36.5	$27.4
	Narrow	44.8	21.4	16.1
Musgraves	Broad	73.9	35.3	26.5
	Narrow	38.4	18.4	13.8
Table 3	Broad	77.1	36.9	27.7
	Narrow	46.6	22.3	16.7

Source: CRS computations based on tables 1–3 and aggregate personal consumption figures from Data Resources, Inc. *Review of the U.S. Economy*, May 1993. p. 9.

Replacement Tax

Some or all of the revenue from a value-added tax could be used to reduce or replace another tax. If the VAT replaces another tax, estimated *gross* revenue would be the same as if the VAT was a new revenue source. *Gross* revenue per 1-percent VAT would vary depending on the broadness of the tax base. Thus, for FY95, estimated *gross* revenue per 1-percent VAT as a replacement tax would be the same dollar amounts for different sources and types of tax bases as shown in table 4.

The dollar amount of VAT needed to replace each dollar of another tax, however, would vary dramatically depending on the tax replaced. Since the VAT is an indirect business tax, if the revenue from a VAT replaces the revenue from some other indirect business tax (that is, excise taxes, customs duties, and miscellaneous receipts), then each dollar of VAT revenue would replace a dollar of revenue of another indirect business tax.

The revenue from a VAT could be used to replace the revenue from a direct tax (that is, individual income tax, corporate income tax, or payroll tax). But for legislative purposes, more than one dollar of gross VAT revenue would be needed to replace each dollar of a direct tax because, under the revenue estimating convention, the VAT would reduce factor incomes, and thus, revenue from direct taxes. The following examples illustrate this concept.

For FY95, CBO's baseline predicts that individual income tax revenue will be $567 billion. If rates were cut in half and the revenue loss made up by imposing a VAT, how large would the VAT need to be to replace the net revenue loss of $283.5 billion? Cutting the rates in half would also cut the individual income tax offset by half and thus reduce the total offset to 16 cents per dollar of VAT (that is, .18/2 + .02 + .05 = .16). Thus, replacing $283.5 billion in revenue from the individual income tax would require gross VAT revenue of $337.5 billion [$283.5 billion / (1 − .16)]. Replacing *all* revenue from the individual income tax would reduce the offset to 7 cents per dollar of VAT. Thus, the replacement of $567 billion in individual income tax would require gross VAT revenue of $609.7 billion [$567 billion / (1 − .07)].

LIMITATIONS OF ESTIMATES

These revenue estimates for a value–added tax are only approximations that depend on revenue estimating conventions and the economic forecast. Actual revenue could be higher or lower.

Reasons for Higher Estimates

There are at least three reasons revenue estimates could be higher. *First*, these revenue estimates were based on the assumption that the only special tax treatment was zero–rating at the retail stage, but products could be exempted. A seller of an exempt product at the retail stage would not charge VAT on its sales, but it would not receive a rebate for VAT paid on its inputs. Thus, the VAT would partially tax the product. A seller of an exempt product at an intermediate stage of production would not charge VAT on sales and would not receive a rebate for VAT paid. The firm at the next stage of production would use the exempt product as an input and charge VAT on its sales. Thus, the exempt product would be taxed more than once, that is, the VAT would cascade. Hence, exempting rather than zero–rating products would raise revenue from a VAT. In developed nations, exemption is more frequently used than zero–rating.[11]

Second, the VAT would partially tax the underground economy which consists primarily of working "off the books" and/or illegal activities. Estimates of the magnitude of the underground economy vary widely depending on its definition and the method of measurement.[12]

Third, tax auditors can compare information about a VAT with information about
business income taxation which would likely increase compliance with both types of taxes. For example, the sales revenue figure reported on business income tax forms may be checked for consistency with gross VAT collected as shown on VAT forms. Also, a check of cash receipts during a VAT audit may identify the underreporting of sales. The firm may attempt not only to evade the VAT but also to evade the business income tax.[13]

---

[11] For a presentation of products which are frequently exempted or zero–rated in developed nations, see: Tait, p. 49–107.

[12] For an overview of the underground economy, see: Carson, Carol S. The Underground Economy: An Introduction. *Survey of Current Business*, v. 64, no. 5, May 1984. p. 21–37.

[13] *Taxing Consumption*. Paris, Organization for Economic Co-operation and Development, 1988. p. 199–200.

Reasons for Lower Estimates

At least three factors would lower actual revenues from a value-added tax. *First*, administrative costs of the VAT would reduce the net revenue from a VAT. Administrative costs would depend on the complexity of the VAT. In 1984, the Department of the Treasury estimated that administering a VAT in the United States would cost approximately $700 million.[14] For 1988, the Congressional Budget Office estimated the administrative cost of a U.S. VAT would be between $750 million and $1.5 billion.[15] For 1995, the General Accounting Office (GAO) estimated the cost of administering a U.S. VAT would be $1.22 billion if the VAT has a single rate, a broad base, and an exemption for business with gross receipts of less than $100,000.[16] In addition, for 1995, the GAO estimated transition costs of approximately $800 million.[17] But, if the VAT is a replacement tax instead of a new revenue source, part of the VAT administrative costs might be offset by savings the administrative costs of the replaced tax.

Second, any tax evasion would reduce the estimated revenue from a VAT. The more complicated the VAT, the more difficult it would be to enforce. The Congressional Budget Office has assumed that a U.S. VAT would have a compliance rate of 95 percent.[18]

Third, these estimates do not take into account the possible shifts in consumption patterns that might be expected if some items are taxed and others are not. If consumers substitute untaxed items for taxed items, the estimated revenue from a VAT would decline. The higher the VAT tax rate, the greater would be the expected substitution of untaxed goods for taxed goods.

In summary, the revenue estimates in this report should be considered as approximations. The actual revenue yields would vary depending on the complexity and structure of the VAT.

---

[14] U.S. Department of the Treasury. Office of the Secretary. *Tax Reform for Fairness, Simplicity, and Economic Growth. Value–Added Tax.* Volume 3. Washington, November 1984. p. 124.
[15] U.S. Congressional Budget Office. *Effects of Adopting a Value–Added Tax.* p. 69.
[16] U.S. General Accounting Office. *Value–Added Tax: Administrative Costs Vary With Complexity and Number of Business.* Washington, May 1993. p. 63.
[17] Ibid., p. 85.
[18] U.S. Congressional Budget Office. *Effects of Adopting a Value–Added Tax.* Washington, February 1992. p. 22.

BIBLIOGRAPHY

Barham, Vicky, S. N. Poddar, and John Whalley. The tax treatment of insurance under a consumption type, destination basis VAT. National tax journal, v. 40, no. 2, June 1987. p. 171–182.

Beaman, Walter H., et al. Technical problems in designing a broad–based value–added tax for the United States. A report of the Special Committee on the Value–Added Tax Section of the American Bar Association. Tax lawyer, v. 28, no. 2, Winter 1975. p. 193–220.

Carson, Carol S. The underground economy: an introduction. Survey of current business, vol. 64, no. 5, may 1984: 21–37.

Data Resources, Inc. Review of the U.S. economy, April 1993. p. 9.

Due, John F. Some unresolved issues in design and implementation of value–added taxes. National tax journal, v. 43, no. 4, December 1990. p. 383–394.

Focus on the value–added tax. Coopers & Lybrand. Washington, 1986. 34 p.

Gillis, Malcolm, Carl S. Shoup, and Gerardo P. Sicat, eds. Value–added taxation in developing countries. Washington, World Bank, 1990. 237 p.

Henderson, Yolanda K. Financial intermediaries under value–added taxation. New England economic review, Federal Reserve Bank of Boston, July/August 1988. p. 37–50.

Hoffman, Lorey Arthur, S. N. Poddar, and John Whalley. Taxation of banking services under a consumption type, destination basis VAT. National tax journal, v. 40, no. 4, December 1987. p. 547–554.

McLure, Charles E. The value–added tax: key to deficit reduction. American Enterprise Institute, Washington, 1987. 184 p.

Musgrave, Richard A., and Peggy B. Musgrave. Public finance in theory and practice. 4th ed. New York, McGraw–Hill, 1984. 824 p.

Tait, Alan A. Value–added tax: international practice and problems. International Monetary Fund, Washington, 1988. 450 p.

Taxing consumption. Paris, Organization for Economic Co–operation and Development, 1988. 335 p.

The role of tax reform in central and eastern European economies. Paris, Organization for Economic Co–operation and Development, 1991. 458 p.

Turner, William J. Designing an efficient value–added tax. Tax law review, v. 39, no. 2, Summer 1984. p. 435–472.

U.S. Congress. Joint Committee on Taxation. Discussion of revenue estimation methodology and process. Washington, U.S. Govt. Print. Off., 1992. 22 p.

U.S. Congressional Budget Office. Effects of adopting a value-added tax. Washington, February 1992. 79 p.

U.S. General Accounting Office. Value-added tax: administrative costs vary with complexity and number of businesses. Washington, May 1993. 159 p.

U.S. Library of Congress. Congressional Research Service. Value-added tax: concepts, policy issue, and OECD experiences, by James M. Bickley. [Washington] 1992. 49 p. CRS Report No. 92-938 E

----- Value-added tax as a new revenue source, by James M. Bickley. [Washington] 1991. (Updated regularly) CRS Issue Brief No. IB91078

U.S. Department of the Treasury. Office of the Secretary. Tax reform for fairness, simplicity, and economic growth. Value-added tax. vol. 3. Washington, November 1984. 128 p.

Value-added taxes: a comparative analysis. Tax Executives Institute, Washington, 1992. 141 p.

INDEX

A

addition method, 4, 34, 89, 90
administrative cost(s), 3, 5, 6, 8, 10-14, 19, 21, 62, 64, 66, 71-73, 77, 90, 91, 93, 100, 109, 111
Advisory Commission on Intergovernmental Relations (ACIR), 31, 54, 55
audited, 64, 66
Australia, 3, 8, 10, 36, 73, 89

B

balance–of–payments, 27
balance–of–trade, 3, 26, 27, 77
broad–based VAT, 2, 8-10, 18, 24, 90, 97, 102
broad–based, national–level consumption tax, 1
Brookings Institution, 19, 20, 30, 59, 61
budget deficits, 1, 83, 84
Bush Administration, 64, 72
Bush, President, 58, 59, 64, 72
business income tax(es), 13, 15, 108
business saving, 24

C

Canadian VAT, 83-85, 88-90, 93-95
capital inputs, 3, 63, 65, 89
capital purchases, 3, 65, 89, 98
Committee on Energy and Commerce, 80
Committee on Finance, 70, 81
compliance costs, 5, 11, 19, 21, 30, 61, 84, 87, 90, 91, 92, 93, 94, 95
Congressional Budget Office (CBO), 9, 10, 16-18, 24, 25, 61, 97, 99, 101, 106, 107, 109, 111
consumer goods, 23, 75
consumers, 1, 26, 28, 64, 66, 68, 71, 73, 76, 83, 84, 86, 87, 91, 109
consumption based tax system, 64, 72
consumption tax, ix, 11, 16, 28, 62, 63, 68-70, 72, 80, 81, 97
consumption taxes, ix, 1, 7, 10, 30, 71, 74, 88
consumption VAT, 3, 63-65, 67, 89, 98, 101
corporate income taxes, 10, 27, 69, 81, 97
credit method, 4, 20, 63-67, 89, 92, 93

credit–invoice method, 4, 5, 13, 31, 89, 90, 98

D

Data Resources, Inc. (DRI), 102, 106, 110
Date Certain Tax Code Replacement Act, 70, 81
deductible expenses, 5
deficit reduction, 2, 8, 10, 11, 60, 78, 110
destination principle, 26, 76
direct tax(es), 8, 26, 98, 107
disposable income, 1, 16, 17, 18, 22, 74, 75, 91
domestic services, 9, 100, 103
double taxation, 64, 66

E

economic decisions, 2, 71, 75
economic efficiency, 11, 20
economic entity, 26
economies of scale, 13
efficiency, 8, 15, 60
equity, 3, 8, 9, 16-19, 23, 60, 71, 73-75, 101
Equity, v, 16, 17, 18, 22, 74
European Community (EC), 9, 13, 19, 20, 26, 60
exempt business, 5, 100
exempt firms, 7
exempt manufacturer, 6
exempt retailer, 6
exempt small businesses, 11
exempt, 5-7, 10, 11, 15, 23, 67, 75, 90, 100, 108
exemption certificates, 67
exemption threshold, 12, 13
exemption, 5, 7, 11-13, 21, 67, 78, 90, 100, 108, 109
expansionary monetary policy, 25, 72, 73, 76

expense per dollar of VAT, 11, 77
exports, 26, 27, 76, 77

F

factors of production, 3, 25, 34, 63, 65, 76, 84
Fair Tax Act of 2001, 69, 80
federal budget, 2, 57, 58, 97, 98
federal consumption tax, 64, 65
federal credit system, 21
Federal Government, 2, 16, 20, 25, 29, 30, 54, 55
federal income tax, 64, 72
federal sales tax (FST), 83, 85-88, 93, 94, 96
Federal Sales Tax Review Committee, 85
Federal VAT, 2, 21, 28, 29, 30, 95
Finance and Economic Affairs Committee, 85
flexible exchange rate system, 27
food stamp entitlements, 22
free trade agreement, 83, 84, 95
Freedom and Fairness Restoration Act of 2001, 69, 70, 80, 81

G

General Accounting Office (GAO), 2, 11-13, 28, 62, 109, 111
General Agreement on Tariffs and Trade (GATT), 26, 27
general consumption tax, 1, 83, 84
general sales taxes, 8, 29, 66
good or service, 3, 65, 84
government saving, 24
gross domestic product (GDP), 79, 99
gross product VAT, 3, 63, 65, 89
gross receipts, 11, 12, 29, 109

H

Harris Poll, 31, 58, 59, 60

High income households, 18, 75
horizontal equity, 16, 22
House Committee on Ways and Means., 69, 70, 80, 81
House of Commons Standing Committee, 85

I

import duties, 8, 37
import(s), 8, 15, 26, 27, 37, 44, 76, 77
income effect, 23, 24, 77
income tax credit(s), 2, 19, 20, 21, 75, 92
income tax liability, 20, 71, 92
income taxes, 8, 10, 20, 24, 25, 29, 54, 55, 58
income tested transfers, 21
income VAT, 3, 63, 65, 89
income-credit system, 88, 92, 93, 94
indirect business tax, 98, 99, 107
individual income taxes, 2, 8, 24, 29, 30, 31, 54, 55
Individual Tax Freedom Act of 2001, 69, 81
intergovernmental relations, 21, 54, 57, 59, 78, 94
intermediate producer, 6
Internal Revenue Code, 70, 81
Internal Revenue Service, 13, 60, 77
international economic stability, 27

J

joint tax collections, 66

L

lifetime income, 17, 18, 75
low taxable incomes, 22
lower income households, 18, 19

M

major revenue sources, 23, 75
manufacturers' sales taxes, 8
Media General/Associated Press, 31, 57, 58, 60
monetary policy, 25, 76
multiple (tax) rates, 2, 4, 5, 15, 19, 20, 75, 90-92, 94

N

narrow–based VAT, 9, 10, 90, 97, 98, 100, 101
National Commission on Tax Reform and Simplification, 70, 81
National Health Care Trust Fund., 79
National Health Insurance Act, 79
national health insurance, 79, 83, 84, 97, 98
national sales tax (NST), 30, 31, 54, 55, 57, 58, 62-68, 101, 102
national saving, 24, 77
neutral tax, 2, 71
nondeductible expenses, 5
nonexempt wholesaler, 6, 7
non–exempt, 7

O

OECD nations, 8, 9
Organization for Economic Cooperation and Development (OECD), 1, 3, 4, 7-10, 13-15, 20, 25, 28, 59, 61, 73, 74, 79, 89, 90, 95, 96, 111
origin principle, 26

P

permanent income, 17
personal consumption, 16, 74, 101-103, 106

personal income tax(es), 10, 18, 24, 29, 57, 58, 78, 97, 99
personal savings rate, 24
preferential tax treatment, 87
private economic decisions, 23, 86
profits on public fiscal monopolies, 8, 37
progressive taxation, 18, 75, 91
public sector, 2, 10, 27, 28, 68
public services, 28
purchase invoice, 5, 13, 32, 99

R

rebatable, 26
reduction in taxes, 10, 97
registered taxpayer, 6, 91, 100
retail sales taxe(s) (RST(s)), 2, 8, 19, 21, 29, 30, 67, 69, 80, 81, 84, 85, 94, 95
retail vendors, 65
revenue estimates, 8-10, 97, 102
revenue source, 1, 2, 10, 29, 62, 71, 83, 84, 97-99, 102, 106, 107, 109, 111
revenue yield, 3, 8, 10, 28, 71-73, 77

S

sales invoice, 4, 5, 13, 31, 32, 90, 99
sales revenue, 15, 108
self-enforcing procedure, 67, 68
Simplified USA Tax Act of 2001, 69, 80
single–rate VAT, 18, 22
size of government, 10, 27, 28, 71, 73, 78
social security taxes, 8, 10, 97, 99
social spending, 2, 19, 75, 92
stage of production, 3, 6, 31, 32, 65, 68, 83, 84, 90, 91, 100, 108
stand–alone credit system, 20, 92
standard rate of taxation, 13
state sales tax, 28, 30

substitution effect, 23, 24, 77
subtraction method, 4, 5, 33, 62, 85, 89
Sweden, 8, 10, 11, 14, 31, 37, 40, 79

T

tax auditor(s), 4, 13, 15, 90, 108
tax authorities, 5, 15, 28, 66, 67, 90, 100
tax base, 8, 19, 30, 64-66, 73, 78, 85, 90, 94, 97, 100, 101, 107
tax complexity, 13, 93
tax credits, 20
tax economists4,, 16, 19, 74, 88, 91, 92, 94, 95
tax information, 15, 66
taxable, 7, 15, 22, 65, 87, 93, 105
transfer payments, 19, 75, 92

U

U.S. balance–of–trade, 2, 27
U.S. Internal Revenue Service, 10
underground economy, 15, 108, 110
United Kingdom, 10, 11, 14, 19, 37, 40, 43, 44, 79
unregistered suppliers, 15
untaxed goods, 23, 72, 76, 83, 86, 109

V

value–added tax (VAT), 1-35, 38-41, 44, 54, 59-69, 71-80, 83-95, 97-102, 105-111
VAT liability, 3, 4, 14, 63, 65, 67, 89, 90
vertical equity, 16, 74

W

wholesale sales taxes, 8

Z

zero–rat(e)ing, 5, 6, 7, 10, 19, 20, 26, 44, 90, 91, 100, 101, 108

zero–rated business, 6, 100
zero–rated manufacturer, 7
zero–rated retailer, 6, 100